LOOKING BACK AT BRITAIN

HOLIDAYS
AND
HARD TIMES

1870s

HOLIDAYS
AND
HARD TIMES

1870s

Jeremy Harwood

 Reader's Digest | gettyimages

CONTENTS

1870s IMAGE GALLERY

FRONT COVER: Two river men working on their boat on the Thames in 1877, a scene from *Street Life in London*.

BACK COVER: Mr A W Burton poses astride his penny-farthing bicycle, a popular mode of transport in the Victorian era. The first penny-farthing appeared in 1870.

TITLE PAGE: Two Victorian bill stickers in a scene from *Street Life in London*, 1877.

OPPOSITE: A trio of middle-class Victorian teenagers, with Jack Russell dog. Girls wore similar fashions to their mothers, but skirts were shorter and less cumbersome.

FOLLOWING PAGES:

Holidaymakers on the beach at Great Yarmouth, Norfolk, in about 1875

A picnic party at Stonehenge, including Queen Victoria's youngest son, Prince Leopold, in 1877.

Three generations of shoeblacks, in a scene from *Street Life in London*, 1877.

A group of civilian scientists aboard HMS *Challenger*, which set sail from Portsmouth in December 1872 on a four-year mission to map the oceans.

THE **WAY WE LIVE NOW**

The 1870s seemed to bode well for Britain. The Queen, still immured in personal grief, had nonetheless presided over an era of unparalleled peace, prosperity and progress since becoming a widow almost a decade earlier. And for the next few years, trade and industry would continue to expand at a tremendous rate.

FAMILY VALUES A prosperous middle-class family pose at their front door with their two maids in 1875.

MONEY AND SOCIETY

Britain's exports of coal, iron, steel, textiles and industrial machinery were reaching all-time highs as the decade began, while shipbuilding expanded proportionately to provide the new ships required to carry the vast increase in foreign trade. Income tax stood at just 4d in the pound (less than 2 per cent) and was levied only on people earning more than £150 a year – a sum way beyond the reach of most ordinary folk. According to the personal columns of *The Times*, a 'good, plain cook' could expect to be paid between £25 and £30 a year, while a 'neat respectable housemaid able to wait well at table' could earn £18, plus, of course, her beer money.

Yet all was not as untroubled as it seemed. Though many workers fought for and won higher wages and shorter working days, the boom of the decade's early years came to an abrupt end largely because of the beginnings of serious foreign competition. Earnings fell dramatically and in the industrial areas many were thrown out of work. To make matters worse, farmers now faced several years of bad harvests in succession and their economic woes were compounded by the mass import of cheaper wheat from the USA, Canada and Australia. From mid-decade on, hard times were back with a vengeance.

Trollope's attack on society

In this climate the popular novelist Anthony Trollope – hitherto best known for his richly comic portrayals of cathedral feuds, provincial town life and country house society – published *The Way We Live Now*, a savage satire on a society that, in his view, had become morally degraded. The England that Trollope now chose to depict had sold its soul to Mammon and turned to a new creed of money worship, as epitomised in the way that his fictional high society fawns on the swindling financier Augustus Melmotte, until his eventual exposure and downfall.

Despite critical praise by contemporaries, some of whom regarded the novel as Trollope's finest, *The Way We Live Now* did not sell well. Perhaps there were too many uncomfortable home truths in what he was saying. No less a personage than the great Liberal leader William Ewart Gladstone would later complain, in 1879, of 'men of rank, men of titles … giving their names to speculations, which they neither understand nor examine, as directors or trustees'. And Lord Robert Cecil,

continued on page 20

BOATING IN THE BLOOD
Spectators pose for the camera in a break from watching the rowers in action. Not only did Victorian Britons work hard, they also played hard when they got the chance and boating was an increasingly popular pastime. By the 1870s, it was already the custom in some industries to give workers Saturday afternoons off. The decade saw a substantial reduction in working hours to around nine per day and the introduction of statutory Bank Holidays.

THE DEATH AND LEGACY OF CHARLES DICKENS

PORTRAIT OF AN AUTHOR

Waterloo Day was usually cause for national celebration. But on 18 June, 1870, the mood was sombre. On that day Charles Dickens, the greatest British novelist of the era, was buried in Westminster Abbey. Dickens had died at the age of 58, worn out by constant overwork. In addition to his prolific novel-writing, he pursued a punishing schedule of public readings, which delighted audiences at home and in the USA. His last novel, *The Mystery of Edwin Drood*, he left unfinished.

The grave selected for the great man was hard by Poet's Corner. Dean Stanley, who conducted the brief funeral service early that morning, had ordered the grave to be left unsealed. All day long, a stream of mourners filed slowly past. People were still paying their respects as midnight approached. The essayist Walter Bagehot commented: 'No other Englishman had attained such a hold on the vast populace.'

Dickens was a truly remarkable man and his unconventional background fed into his

books. The son of a government clerk who was imprisoned for debt in the Marshalsea Prison, the young Charles had next to no schooling. He was practically penniless when, as a young man, he began to report on Parliamentary debates for the *Monthly Magazine*. Then in 1838 came the launch of *The Pickwick Papers*: it was a smash hit. Year after year, masterpieces poured from his pen; *Bleak House, A Christmas Carol, David Copperfield, Dombey and Son, Great Expectations, Hard Times, Nicholas Nickleby, Oliver Twist* – all captivated the reading public as they appeared.

The photograph of Dickens reading to his two daughters (left) was taken in the garden of Gad's Hill, his home in Kent, in the late 1860s. The caricature below sums up his state of constant busy-ness. The illustrations show, from top to bottom, Oliver Twist daring to ask for a more, Mr Gradgrind in a scene from *Hard Times* and Dolly Varden, a character in *Barnaby Rudge*. Dickens invented more than 2,000 such characters.

NOT-SO-POPULAR VOICE
The English novelist Anthony Trollope in 1875, the year that his 20 monthly instalments for *The Way We Live Now* were gathered together and published in novel form. For a public eager to read more of Barchester or the Pallisers, Trollope's latest offering was less to their liking. It shone an unflattering light on certain aspects of Victorian society and some of its more dubious money-making practices. It was not that Trollope disapproved of money. On the contrary, his upbringing and personal circumstances gave him a keen appreciation of its importance, and he has been described as the Victorian author with the greatest knowledge of finance. Greed, dishonesty and irresponsible speculation were the targets of his satire.

rising star of the Conservatives who would, as Marquis of Salisbury, succeed Disraeli as leader, even anticipated the great novelist. Before the publication of Trollope's novel in 1875, Cecil went on record as despising 'that money-worshipping, grovelling, materialistic spirit so rapidly increasing amongst us'.

The gulf between the very rich and the extremely poor, always broad in Victorian times, was widening. Fortunately for the country, old-fashioned common sense, the gradual implementation of some much-needed social reforms and the continuing rise of a relatively prosperous middle class combined to save the situation. There would be no British equivalent of the Paris Commune, the worker's rising that came close to destroying much of the French capital in the aftermath of France's defeat in the Franco-Prussian War.

For many people, the money-making derided by Trollope did not require any apology. Quite the contrary, it was something to be proud of and enthusiastically encouraged. This was why Samuel Smiles' *Self Help*, with its heady gospel of self-reliance and self-improvement, was one of the best-sellers of the day. For thousands of aspiring readers, it was the potential key to bettering their lot in life.

TOY MENAGERIE
The young child of a well-to-do Victorian family poses with a Noah's ark toy set. As well as familiar creatures, the set includes giraffes, peacocks, camels and elephants, reflecting the Victorian fascination with exotic animals. The gap between rich and poor widened as the 1870s progressed, and the contrast was nowhere more visible than in the relative situations of children. But just because a child came from a rich family did not mean that he or she was pampered. Their place was firmly in the nursery, under the tutelage of a governess and nursery maid. Most Victorians considered physical punishment essential in the training of children and conditions for boys at public school were tough by anyone's standards.

NO PLACE LIKE HOME

Victorians of this period shared an almost fanatical devotion to home life. *The Home Circle*, *The Home Companion*, *The Home Friend*, *Home Thought*, *Family Economist* and *Family Record* were just a few of the magazines that sprang up at this time. Composer Sir Henry Bishop's 'Home Sweet Home', with sentimental words by John Howard Payne, may have been written half a century earlier, but it had now become a firm family favourite, sung around the piano of an evening in countless drawing rooms, sitting rooms and parlours the length and breadth of the land. According to one contemporary commentator, it achieved the status of 'almost our national melody.' Lord and Lady Folkestone chose to be painted, by the artist Edward Clifford, singing the song standing beside their eldest son.

An orgy of house building was transforming towns and cities, while grand country houses were 'improved' or new ones sprang up, usually in the fashionable neo-Gothic style. Prices for middle-class houses varied, then as now, according to size and location. According to *The Times* in the mid-1870s, a substantial eight-bedroom house in leafy Hampton Court, convenient for town and the amenities of the river, cost £1,900 freehold. An alternative was to rent it at £90 a year. In out-of-town Barnet in Hertfordshire, by comparison, a three-bedroom villa could be purchased freehold for 300 guineas, or rented for £65 per annum.

Suburbs sprawled as towns and cities expanded. Many writers, including a Mrs Panton, a popular journalist and pioneer of the notion of 'interior design,' sung the praises of these new developments. She urged 'young people' without too much money to up sticks and look to moving to a home 'some little way out of London'. There, she wrote: 'rents are less; smuts and blacks [flakes of soot] are conspicuous by their absence; a small garden or even a tiny conservatory is not an impossibility; and if the man of the house has to pay for his season-ticket, that is nothing in comparison with his being able to sleep in fresh air; to have a game of tennis in summer, or a friendly evening of music, chess, or games in the winter, without expense.' *The Builder* magazine concurred: 'Railways and omnibuses are plentiful and it is better, morally and physically, for the Londoner, when he has done his day's work, to go to the country or the suburbs, where he escapes the noise, the crowds and impure air of the town; and it is no small advantage for a man to have his family removed from the immediate neighbourhood of casinos, dancing saloons, and hells upon earth which we will not name.'

There was a plethora of choice in other cities, too. For the well-to-do, the Midlands had Edgbaston, planned to provide 'genteel homes for the middle classes' and hailed as the 'Belgravia of Birmingham'. It housed the families who owned the industries on which the town thrived, but who did not want to live too near them. Glasgow had its Kelvinside, Edinburgh its Morningside.

In London, suburbs were ranked to keep the classes separate. Camberwell and Peckham – that 'bow'r' and 'Arcadian Vale' as W S Gilbert called them in *Trial by Jury* in 1875 – were particularly favoured by lower middle class clerks thanks to the London & South Eastern Railway, which whisked them speedily into the heart of the bustling City. Hammersmith, Balham and Leyton were also all recognised as lower middle class domains. Penge and Ealing – both, at the time, without direct rail links to town – were deemed middle class. Hampstead was upper middle. St John's Wood was home to authors, journalists and publishers, while Haverstock Hill, Brixton, Clapham, Kennington and Stockwell were the chosen areas of what were termed 'City men'. Highgate, Sydenham, Barnes and Richmond were the jealously guarded preserves of the rich.

> 'After my work in the City, I like to be at home. What's the good of a home if you are never in it? "Home Sweet Home", that's my motto.'
>
> Charles Pooter in *The Diary of a Nobody*, 1888

Palaces in the country

It cost on average between £7,000 and £10,000 to erect what was deemed to be a 'proper' country house, but many spent far more than that on their country seat, as at Eaton Hall, the Cheshire home of the Dukes of Westminster. The architect Alfred Waterhouse reshaped the existing building, designed for the Duke's grandfather, into an immense neo-Gothic edifice. He made the already large house

STATELY HOME

Eaton Hall in Cheshire (left), the country seat of the Dukes of Westminster, had been owned by the Grosvenor family since the reign of Henry VI. The house itself had been rebuilt several times over the centuries. In the 1870s, the first Duke (top right) decided to expand it still further. As the richest man in the country, he could afford to build on the grandest scale. The architect Charles Waterhouse responded by creating for him a masterpiece of Victorian Gothic. This contemporary view shows the garden front, with the main block of the house on the left and the family wing on the far right. The linking wing contained extra guest accommodation. The celebrated clock tower was intended to look like Big Ben.

INNOVATIVE CLIENT

Industrialist Lord Armstrong (bottom right) was another far-sighted builder of the period. Having made his fortune in armaments, founding the Armstrong-Vickers factory in Newcastle-Upon-Tyne, he commissioned the celebrated architect Norman Shaw to transform Cragside, his Northumberland country home. The work took 15 years to complete, from 1869 to 1884, and when finished it was the ultimate word in modernity – the first house in the world to be totally powered by electricity. The power was supplied by a hydroelectric plant of Armstrong's own devising in the Cragside grounds. Armstrong also ordered the planting of 7 million trees and shrubs creating a wooded vale to surround his dream home.

larger still by adding a private wing – to which the Duke and Duchess could retire when not entertaining, a chapel – a domestic wing big enough for a small army of servants, a stable block and new coach houses. By the time Waterhouse had finished, the massive construction resembled a medieval Gothic cathedral.

Despite costing over £600,000 (around £32.5 million today), the clients were delighted with what Waterhouse had accomplished. As intended, Eaton Hall had become by far the biggest house in the neighbourhood, requiring 50 indoor servants to run it efficiently. The dining room was large enough to seat 60 guests without overcrowding. There were 150 bedrooms, and though the bathrooms were relatively few in number, they boasted all the latest in modern amenities.

The newly rich – and, in many cases, the newly ennobled – were not to be left behind. The Rothschild banking family erected no fewer than seven grand houses in the Vale of Aylesbury, setting new standards of opulence and comfort. Their flurry of building led wits to say that Buckinghamshire should be renamed 'Rothschildshire'. In particular, Waddesden Manor was the last word in luxury. It was built by Baron Ferdinand de Rothschild in the mid-1870s to host his summer house parties and to house his renowned collection of art treasures. Designed externally to resemble a Renaissance-style French Loire chateau, internally Waddesden boasted lifts, under-floor central heating and the new electric light.

But Waddesden was not the first private house to be lit by electricity. Up in Northumberland, armaments millionaire Sir William Armstrong had already employed architect Norman Shaw to build him Cragside, a neo-Tudor country home near Rothbury. The house and the 1,729 acres of garden that surrounded it were considered to be one of the architectural wonders of the era. Chinese and Japanese warlords, the Shah of Persia, the Crown Prince of Afghanistan and the King of Siam all came to marvel at Armstrong's extraordinary creation, in which electricity – generated by the house's own hydroelectric plant – lit the rooms, powered the central heating system, turned the spit in the kitchen and even struck the gong to signal mealtimes.

'ONWARD CHRISTIAN SOLDIERS'

Britain was never more religious than in the Victorian era. The middle classes in particular were almost fanatically punctilious in their religious observances. From the Queen downwards, it seemed as if everyone – at least those who counted among the nation's citizens – was a practising believer. As the legal head of the Church of England, the Queen was passionately interested in church matters. She was particularly opposed to the so-called Ritualists, whom, she feared, were steering the Anglican Church back towards Rome with an unwarranted fondness for 'dressings, bowings, incense, Confession and everything of that kind'.

Victoria's enthusiasm for the subject could catch out the unwary. While visiting Balmoral, an alarmed Disraeli sent an urgent telegraph to his secretary: 'Ecclesiastical affairs rage here. Send me Crockford's Directory. I must be armed.' Gladstone found other grounds for complaint. Along with the Archbishop of Canterbury and the Deans of Windsor and Westminster, he objected to the Queen's habit of taking communion in the local kirk, which was conveniently close to the castle. He tried to insist on driving some 15 miles to attend a Scottish Episcopal Church service. 'I do not think Sunday is the best of days here,' he wrote to his wife. 'I in vain enquired, with care, about Episcopal Services.'

In the countryside, practically all villagers attended either church or chapel on Sunday, many of them worshipping two or even three times a day. For the children there was Sunday School. Much the same pattern was followed in the towns and the cities, though in poor areas attendance was far patchier.

Rousing hymns and lengthy sermons were the order of the day. There were new hymns, such as 'Onward Christian Soldiers,' which probably owed its popularity more to its catchy tune, composed in 1871 by Arthur Sullivan, than to its words. Traditionalists clung lovingly to old favourites like 'All Things Bright

SPREADING THE FAITH
For some, preaching the word at home was not enough. Scottish divine Robert Moffat (1795-1883, right) was a pioneer missionary in southern Africa for more than half a century. Mary, his eldest daughter, married David Livingstone, who was to become even more famous than his father-in-law. Moffat spent his missionary years in Bechuanaland (today's Botswana), returning to Britain only twice. On his first visit home, he persuaded the young Livingstone to take up mission work in Africa, rather than in China. In 1870 Moffatt and his wife, also Mary, returned for good and she died the following year. He continued to support his former mission, sending funds towards a training institute there. In 1874 he was called on to identify the body of his son-in-law, who died in 1873 at a village in the Ilala country, at the very heart of the continent. Livingstone's sun-dried body had been brought back to Britain for state burial in Westminster Abbey.

and Beautiful'. As for sermons, the Reverend W W Andrews, a typical Anglican vicar of the time, thought a sermon was not worthy of the name unless it lasted for at least an hour and a quarter. In Birmingham, John Angell James, minister of the Carr Lane Independent Chapel, preached for hours at a stretch, sustaining his voice by sucking the oranges thrown up to him from time to time by members of his flock seated directly under his pulpit.

At home, it was grace before and after meals and normally evening family prayers. After a visit to Lord Northbrook's Hampshire home, William Cory, an Eton schoolmaster, recorded how his host assembled family, guests and servants together in his library at 9.00pm precisely and personally read prayers to them, plus a chapter of whatever he deemed appropriate from the Old Testament.

Sunday observance became almost a religion in itself. All places of entertainment were closed, including museums and art galleries, and no games of

EVANGELICAL LEADER
Bishop Ryle, nominated by Disraeli at the end of the decade to be the first Bishop of Liverpool, stood for all that was best in the Church of England. A leader of the Evangelists within the Church, he wrote more than 200 tracts explaining his views. He had 'a strong conviction that we want more deep-searching study of the Scriptures in the present day. Most Christians see nothing beyond the surface ...'

The Evangelicals formed a powerful faction opposing the so-called Ritualists, who favoured practices that to many – including the Queen – seemed to be allowing Roman Catholic superstitions in via the back door. Matters were not helped when Pope Pius IX proclaimed the doctrine of papal infallibility. The Public Worship Act of 1874 was expressly framed to put an end to Ritualism. Five clergymen were sent to prison for defying its provisions.

any description were allowed. Even the reading of novels was frowned upon – people turned instead to their Bibles or an 'improving' book of sermons.

Saints and sinners

During the decade, various colourful characters emerged to give the established church a wake-up call. In 1874 two American evangelists, Dwight D Moody and Ira D Sankey, embarked on a whirlwind tour of Britain, drawing vast crowds wherever they went. Some poured scorn on their message. A 'London physicist', who chose not to reveal his identity, produced a pamphlet claiming that 'The People Go Mad Through Religious Revivals'. He denounced Moody as 'a third-rate star' and declared Sankey's voice – he led the mass singing – 'decidedly bad'.

AMERICAN VISITORS
The celebrated American Evangelist duo, Dwight Moody (above) and Ira D Sankey (right), toured Britain in 1874-5, spreading their message of hellfire and damnation. For the repentant, they held out the promise of salvation. Their revivalist meetings drew people in their thousands. In Belfast, the local newspaper reported on the 'soul-stirring sight' of 3,000 standing up to sing: 'It was like the sound of many waters to hear this multitude sing the new song in one burst of praise.'

Preachers like Moody and Sankey were in tune with the rapid spread of Nonconformity throughout the nation's industrial heartlands. By 1874, there were an estimated 20,375 chapels of Baptist, Congregational and Methodist denominations in England and Wales alone. The Church of England regarded the Nonconformist phenomenon with suspicion and not a little disdain; the novelist and Anglican cleric Charles Kingsley dismissed Baptist pastors as 'muck enthroned on their respective dunghills'.

Britain came up with its own hell-fire and damnation Revivalist in William Booth, who founded the Salvation Army in 1878 at a so-called 'War Conference' in London's East End. Despite substantial local opposition – primarily from publicans, who were angered by Booth's denunciation of the 'demon drink' – the Salvationists, with their striking uniforms and marching bands, gradually gained a foothold and following across the country.

So-called 'fallen women' were a favourite target of Christian philanthropists, who stalked the streets looking for prostitutes to save from sin. Dr Thomas Barnardo's concern was neglected and abandoned children, probably Victorian London's greatest shame. In 1870, he founded his first home for destitute and homeless children. He was to devote the rest of his life to their cause.

Christian philanthropy undoubtedly had an immense influence. But despite the efforts of people like Lord Shaftesbury to force the government to legislate, charity remained an almost entirely private enterprise. Social welfare was an area in which the state proved stubbornly reluctant to intervene.

STARS AND ENTERTAINMENTS

For the well-off, evenings out meant concerts, the theatre and the opera. The musical highlight of the decade was the visit of German composer Richard Wagner in 1878 to conduct at a month-long festival of his music. In the same year, delighted audiences roared appreciation at the caricature of W H Smith, Disraeli's First Lord of the Admiralty, as Sir Joseph Porter KCB in Gilbert and Sullivan's *HMS Pinafore*. In an era of considerable talent, the stars of the stage were inching towards respectability.

'Not content with being run after on stage, this woman is asked into people's houses to act, and even to luncheon and dinner; and all the world goes. It is an outrageous scandal.'

Lady Frederick Cavendish, on Sarah Bernhardt

LEADING LADIES
French actress Sarah Bernhardt (left) was acclaimed as the star of the century when she played a triumphant London season at the Gaiety Theatre in 1879. Her adoring fans, including the Prince of Wales who had seen her in Paris, flocked to admire 'the divine Sarah'.

Lillie Langtry (right) also had a nickname. She was the 'Jersey Lily', after her Channel Island birthplace. Her beauty stunned society when she arrived in London in 1877. Millais, Whistler and Edward Burne-Jones all painted her. Before long, she became the mistress of the Prince of Wales, who helped to further her career when she decided to go on the stage. The first play she appeared in was Goldsmith's *She Stoops to Conquer*. She is pictured here as Cleopatra in Shakespeare's *Antony and Cleopatra*.

By contrast, Madge Kendall (above), another celebrated actress of the day, was nothing if not respectable. In 1879 she took on the management of the St James's Theatre with her actor husband, and they did much to clean up what went on behind the scenes as well as on stage. Her favourite playwright was the young Arthur Pinero.

LEADING MAN

Charles Wyndham became one of the country's leading actor-managers, specialising in melodramas and popular comedies. Victorian melodramas made great use of dramatic stage effects and were firm audience favourites, but they did not always meet with critical approval. After a performance at the Drury Lane theatre, a critic writing in *The Theatre* expressed the view that 'the great success achieved at Drury Lane certainly justifies Mr Harris [the theatre manager] in his strong opinion that action is vastly more important than dialogue.'

THEATRICAL STAR

Henry Irving (above) was the greatest and best-loved actor of the age, and it was in the 1870s that he came into his own as an acclaimed star. He played Hamlet, Macbeth and Othello during the decade, and in 1878 began his renowned partnership with the equally famous actress Ellen Terry. In 1895 he became the first actor ever to receive a knighthood. When Queen Victoria, for whom Irving staged several Command performances, conferred the accolade, she broke with tradition, saying 'we are very pleased, sir'.

ROYAL ENTERTAINERS

The Jubilee Singers (right) of Fisk University, Nashville, Tennessee, toured Britain in 1873. The highlight of their visit was a concert they performed for the Queen and the royal court. Previously, they had sung at the White House on the invitation of President Ulysses S Grant, the victorious Union general of the American Civil War. All the members of the singing group were former slaves or the children of slaves. Their repertoire included slave songs, spirituals and songs by Stephen Foster, the writer of such popular classics as 'Beautiful Dreamer' and 'Oh Susanna'. The Jubilee Singers were the genuine article, but Foster's songs were more often heard sung by blackface minstrel shows, which were extremely popular in Victorian Britain. White performers used burnt cork, or later greasepaint or shoe polish, to blacken their faces and exaggerate their lips. Woolly wigs, tailcoats or ragged clothes completed the look. The most celebrated troupe of the day was Moore & Burgess's Minstrels, who played regular seasons, year in and year out, at St James's Hall, Piccadilly, for an amazing 35 years.

THE HUMAN CANNONBALL

Zazel was the world's first female human cannonball. The photographs below show her before (left) and after (right) being fired from 'a monstrous cannon' at the Royal Aquarium, London, in 1877.

Zazel's real name was Rosa Matilda Richter and she had trained as an acrobat, which stood her in good stead for her daring new incarnation. At the time of her Royal Aquarium debut, she was just 14 years old. The cannon featured in the show had been specially devised by William Hunt, otherwise known as the Great Fanini, who managed the entertainments at the Aquarium at the time. The cannon relied on rubber springs to catapult the performer into the air, and the distances involved were fairly limited.

After her success at the Royal Aquarium, Zazel went on to tour with P T Barnum's celebrated circus. Sadly, her time with the show came to a sudden and tragic end. During an actual performance she missed the safety net and crashed to the ground, breaking her back. She had to spend the rest of her life in a back brace.

COMIC GENIUS

For 30 years, music hall star Arthur Roberts – seen here as Gentleman Joe, a cab driver – was the idol of what he termed 'London's *jeunesse stage doree*' ('stage-struck golden youth'), who slavishly copied his flamboyant style of dress and retold his saucy jokes. A peerless comic actor and pantomime Dame, Roberts was the despair of writers everywhere because of his incorrigible habit of improvising. Frequently he abandoned the script altogether, completely ignoring the lines penned by the writer.

POSTERS, SCORES AND GAMES

Much of the time, Victorian families made their own entertainment. Family games were extremely popular, such as Harlequin's Rambles (above left), originally devised to publicise a pantomime. For those who could afford one, no drawing room was complete without a piano, tastefully covered – as one writer on home decoration suggested – with serge, felt or damask 'edged with an appropriate fringe'. For amateur singers, there were all sorts of songs to try out, from the latest sentimental ballads and musical monologues to the best-known arias from the popular operas of the day. 'Faust in Five Minutes' (above centre) was a typical example of the latter.

When it came to going out, there was always the theatre and, though not exactly respectable family entertainment, the music hall. They advertised their offerings with lavish posters, like these for the Metropole Theatre and Opera House in Camberwell (far left) and the Empire Theatre of Varieties in Brighton (left). The Egyptian Hall in London's Piccadilly (above) was a one-off. Built in 1812 to house a natural history collection, by the 1870s it had hosted an eclectic variety of attractions. It ended up the headquarters of the great magicians and illusionists, Maskelyne and Cooke.

PEACE AND REFORM

It had been a white Christmas and it was to get colder as the New Year of 1870 dawned. Most people, though, were not put off by the inclement weather. They were too busy anticipating what the future might bring. The nation was prospering and a new reforming government, headed by the redoubtable William Ewart Gladstone, was firmly in power.

MATURE STATESMAN William Ewart Gladstone, four-time Prime Minister of Britain, photographed in 1875 shortly after his first term in power.

GLADSTONE AND IRELAND

At the General Election towards the end of 1868, Gladstone's talismanic oratory had won the Liberals a landslide victory over Benjamin Disraeli and the Conservatives. But just as things seemed set fair for the future, storm clouds began to loom from Europe. Even though Britain played no part in the actual conflict, the Franco-Prussian War of 1870-1 was to radically alter the balance of power and shake the Continent to its foundations.

Meanwhile, at home, the country was forced to come face to face with growing Irish discontent at the continuance of British rule. From the moment Gladstone received the news that he was to be called upon to form a new government, he had no doubt about his foremost priority. 'My mission', he said to Evelyn Ashley, a house guest at Hawarden Castle, the premier's Flintshire home, 'is to pacify Ireland.' To fulfil this pledge Gladstone proposed to disestablish the Church of Ireland and reform the Irish land and educational systems. He succeeded in the first of these tasks, but in the other two he failed.

Raising the Irish Question

The official Church of Ireland was Anglican, while the overwhelming majority of the people were Roman Catholic. The need to end this Anglican supremacy had been one of Gladstone's chief rallying cries in the election that swept him back to power. In a keynote campaign speech in Wigan, he made his intentions clear. He compared the Protestant ascendancy in Catholic Ireland to 'Some tall tree of noxious growth, lifting its head to Heaven and poisoning the atmosphere of the land so far as its shadow can extend. It is still there, gentlemen, but now at last the day has come when, as we hope, the axe has been laid to the root.'

The audience responded with cheers, which grew ever louder as Gladstone continued: 'There lacks, gentlemen, but one stroke more – the stroke of these elections. It will then, once for all, topple to its fall, and, on that day, the heart of Ireland will leap for joy, and the mind and conscience of England and Scotland will repose with thankful satisfaction upon the thought that something has been done towards the discharge of national duty, and towards deepening and widening the foundations of public strength, security and peace.'

continued on page 42

'Ireland is at your doors. Providence placed her there; law and Legislature have made a compact between you; you must face these obligations; you must deal with them and discharge them.'

William Gladstone, speaking at an election rally in 1868

THE LAND ACT
Local men pose for the camera in the Irish village of Duagh on Achill Island, County Mayo. As economic conditions worsened in the 1870s, discontent against British rule grew, particularly in the countryside. Most Irish farmers were tenants, at the mercy of demands made on them by their often absentee landlords. They called for action to put an end to the constant threat of eviction that they faced if they fell behind with paying their rents.

Though Gladstone confessed himself to be 'a good deal staggered at the idea of any interference with present rents', he decided that the tenants should have some protection against unfair treatment. His Land Act was the result. In it, he attempted to reconcile the demands of the tenants for what they called the 'three Fs' – Fair rents, Fixity of tenure and Free sale' – with those of the landlords, who insisted that the government maintain their property rights.

As Gladstone recorded, it took him 'three months of hectic consultation' to draft the bill, and another three-and-a-half months to personally pilot it through the House of Commons. Opposition was fierce and came from many within his own Liberal party, as well as from the Tories.

LIVING ON THE LAND

William O'Brien (above) was a young journalist whose political ideas were shaped by the Fenian movement. As a founder of the Land League, and later as a Nationalist MP, he espoused the cause of poor Irish tenant farmers, trying to improve their plight.

Some tenant farmers were better off than others. On the farm here, the horses and other well-fed livestock, as well as the sizeable, well-thatched farmhouse, all indicate the family's relative prosperity. In Ulster, when fixing the rent a landlord was obliged to take into account any improvements made by the tenant. Gladstone's Land Act extended this practice to the rest of Ireland, but his legislation stopped short of providing the security of tenure that was the tenant farmers' main demand. It was this omission that fuelled Irish unrest. Many remembered Lord Palmerston's notorious saying, 'tenant's right is landlord's wrong', and feared that in hard times they would be driven off the land if they could not pay whatever their landlords demanded. By the end of the decade, as the agricultural depression bit deep, this fear had become a reality for many. An average of 200 evicted tenant farmers a week were leaving the port of Larne for the USA, while hundreds more were crossing the Irish Sea in search of work in Liverpool and Glasgow.

This was the 'People's William' – as Gladstone had been affectionately nicknamed by the masses – at his oratorical best. Queen Victoria, though, was far from amused. Disraeli had tried to set her mind at rest by assuring her that Gladstone had 'mistaken the spirit of the times and the temper of the country', but this only made the Conservative defeat a more unexpected and unwelcome surprise – 'a strange and unfortunate result', as Disraeli described it. She told her new Prime Minister that although 'she hardly understood the subject as yet, she greatly regretted that he had committed himself to so sweeping a measure'.

Irish land reform

But Gladstone did not stop there. He was also determined to tackle the problems of the thousands of poverty-stricken Irish tenant farmers and so bring an end to the mounting enmity between them and their landlords. That hostility had been growing for years. British legislation in Ireland had deliberately stifled industry in the country, leaving the Irish with only the land to rely upon for their livelihood. And then there were the sheer numbers looking to it for a living. Despite the horrific famines of the 1840s, which through starvation and emigration had reduced Ireland's population by almost 3 million, the population of around 5 million was still larger than the land could support.

What the Irish wanted above all was the chance to own their land. Failing that, tenants should not have to face the peril of summary eviction should they fall behind in paying their rents. Rent, they argued passionately, must be set at a level that they could afford to pay. If the worst came to the worst and they were to be evicted, at the very least they should be compensated for any improvements they had made to their holdings. Gladstone tried to meet some of these demands through a new Land Act, but even some of his cabinet colleagues were horrified by what they saw as an unacceptable attack on landlords and their property rights. Robert Lowe, the irascible Chancellor of the Exchequer, announced that he 'would rather give up everything than consent to put his hand in one man's pocket and rob him for the benefit of another'. Disraeli was even more forthright in his condemnation. After the Act became law, he denounced the Prime Minister for 'shaking property to its foundations, consecrating sacrilege, making government ridiculous and sowing the seeds of civil war'.

It was soon apparent that the Land Act had serious defects. It was relatively easy for landlords to get around its provisions, and the tenants it was intended to benefit realised that it did not give them complete security of tenure. Nor did it protect them against excessive rents. When a major agricultural depression set in in 1875, many tenant farmers were unable to pay any rent at all, and the all-too-familiar cycle of eviction, unrest and consequent coercion began all over again.

Despite all these signs to the contrary, having passed the Land Act Gladstone felt that he had gone as far as was necessary. He delivered a series of passionate denunciations of the emerging Home Rule movement. In September 1871 he told an audience in Scotland: 'So far as my research has gone I have seen nothing, except that it is stated there is a vast quantity of fish in the seas that surround Ireland and that, if they had Home Rule, they would catch a great deal of these fish. But there are fish in the sea which surrounds England and Scotland. England has no Home Rule, and Scotland has no Home Rule, but we manage to catch the fish!' His listeners responded with cheers and laughter. A further decade was to pass before Gladstone became a convert to the necessity of Irish Home Rule.

'The sergeant was describing a military life. It was all drinking, he said, except that there were frequent intervals of eating and love-making ...'

Charles Dickens

GUN PRACTICE
Young British soldiers pose with a field gun and an ammunition limber in an Irish military camp in the early 1870s. Though the numbers fluctuated widely, up to 26,000 soldiers – a seventh of Britain's regular army – were stationed in Ireland at any given time. Many found life there to their liking, although Dickens' observation perhaps did not apply to all. The general poverty in Ireland made it a fertile recruiting ground. At one time, it was estimated that two-thirds of the British Army consisted of Irishmen or soldiers of Irish descent.

A PRINCE AT OXFORD
Prince Leopold, Duke of Albany (1853-84, seated far right) picnicking at Oxford in June 1874 with his friends (left to right) W J D Campbell, J Lockwood and R H Collins. Leopold, Victoria's youngest son, had pleaded with his reluctant mother to allow him to go to university. The Queen set strict limitations on his conduct. He was limited in the number of men he could invite to dinner and was strictly forbidden to entertain 'any at all of the fairer sex.' The prince told Walter Stirling, his former tutor, that this prohibition was 'a great pity, as there are such awfully pretty girls here, unmarried as well as married'.

THE QUEEN AND HER PEOPLE

As a result of his resolve to try to deal with the Irish problem, Gladstone was embarked on a course of action that would lead to his alienation from the upper classes. Most of them came to detest both him and his political views, which they believed posed a dangerous threat to the stability of Victorian society. Later in his career he delighted in castiga~ting what he called 'the upper ten thousand'.

The Queen herself was at their head. She had started off respecting and even liking Gladstone, largely because the Prince Consort had got on well with him and she followed Albert's lead. But now respect turned to distrust, liking to loathing. There were various causes behind her dramatic change of heart, but a primary one

was her deepening resentment at Gladstone's efforts to cajole her into playing a more active part in public life. The Prime Minister had good reason to try. At the start of the 1870s, the Queen was widely unpopular, in large part because of her decade-long self-imposed seclusion. Another factor was her almost constant demands for money to meet the needs of her growing family. The two together had a poisonous effect on public opinion.

Even Sir Henry Ponsonby, the Queen's private secretary, had misgivings. Lord Halifax, the Lord Privy Seal, voiced the Cabinet's concerns to him: 'It is impossible to deny that HM is drawing too heavily on the credit of her former popularity. The mass of the people expect a King or Queen to look and play the part. They want to see a Crown and Sceptre and all that sort of thing. They want the gilding for the money.' Lady Amberley, the daughter of Lord John Russell, noted in her journal: 'Everyone is abusing the Queen very much for not being in London or Windsor … No respect or loyalty seems left in the way people allow themselves to talk of the Queen, saying things like "What do we pay her for if she will not work?" and "She had better abdicate if she is incompetent to do her duty."'

Things went from bad to worse. In 1871 Prince Arthur's coming-of-age sparked off a mass demonstration against 'princely paupers' in Trafalgar Square. The young Liberal MP George Otto Trevelyan fuelled the fires of discontent, anonymously publishing a pamphlet entitled 'What Does She Do with it?' He had calculated that the Queen was squirreling away no less than £200,000 a year out of the monies voted to her by Parliament for her own purposes. Joseph Chamberlain, another rising radical star, told cheering crowds in his home city of Birmingham that a republic was inevitable. And in the House of Commons, the Liberal backbencher and self-declared republican Sir Charles Dilke was cheered when he demanded a public enquiry into the royal finances.

A sea-change of opinion

Then an event occurred that nobody could have anticipated, and it turned popular opinion solidly back in the Queen's favour. On 21 November, 1871, a telegram arrived at Balmoral from Sandringham, the Prince of Wales's country home. It informed the Queen that her 30-year-old son and heir was dangerously ill with typhoid fever – the same illness that had killed his father.

Mother and son had not exactly seen eye to eye for some time. The previous year Edward had narrowly escaped being cited as co-respondent in a divorce case. Though Victoria had believed his assurances that he had not committed adultery with the wife of Sir Charles Mordaunt, she had not hesitated to criticise his 'intimate acquaintance' with a young married woman, which could not fail 'to damage him in the eyes of the middle and lower classes'. She condemned the fast set that Edward called his friend as the 'frivolous, selfish and pleasure-seeking rich'. The people seemed to agree with her. The Prince had been booed at Ascot and hissed at the theatre. Gladstone summed up the mood in a letter to Lord Granville, his closest Cabinet confidante: 'To speak in rude and general terms', he wrote, 'the Queen is invisible and the Prince of Wales is not respected.'

Everything changed as the Queen hastened south to be at her son's bedside. Doctors' bulletins grew in number – on one day alone, five were issued. Probably these were what inspired Alfred Austin, who later was appointed Poet Laureate, to pen the lines:

'Along the wires, the electric message came:
He is no better, he is much the same.'

The Queen herself wrote: 'In those heart-rending moments, I hardly knew how to pray aright, only asking God if possible to spare my Beloved Child.'

CRACK SHOT
The Prince of Wales (left) poses casually with a wild bull he has just killed in the grounds of Chillingham Castle, the Northumberland home of Earl Grey. The Prince was a keen shot. At Sandringham, his country house in Norfolk, he frequently entertained shooting parties during the season (above). Shooting began promptly after breakfast and continued until the day's bag was laid out for the Prince's inspection before being carted off to the royal game larder, said to be the second largest in the world. It needed to be big to hold the enormous quantities of partridge, pheasant, woodcock, wild duck, hares and rabbits that the Prince and his guests killed each year.

The ladies of the house party joined the men for lunch. They were expected to watch the afternoon's sport, though many complained bitterly behind the Prince's back of the extreme cold. The Duchess of Marlborough wrote that, even though she had taken shelter behind a hedge, she was chilled to the marrow by the 'north winds blowing straight from the sea'.

ROYAL RECOVERY
Queen Victoria is pictured holding the order of service and in the dress she wore to attend St Paul's Cathedral on 27 February, 1872, to give thanks for the recovery of the Prince of Wales from a life-threatening attack of typhoid fever. The medal above was struck by the Corporation of London to commemorate the event.

Edward had contracted the disease during a visit to Lord Landesborough's home near Scarborough the previous November. His recovery, after the doctors despaired of saving his life, sparked a dramatic display of public enthusiasm and affection for the royal family, marking the start of the monarchy's recovery from a period of intense unpopularity. There was as much excitement in London on the day of the thanksgiving celebration as there had been almost a decade earlier when Princess Alexandra had arrived for her wedding. On his return to Marlborough House after the ceremony, Edward wrote to his mother to tell her that he could not find the words to express 'how gratified and touched' he was 'by the feeling that was displayed in those crowded streets' towards her and himself.

The crisis came on 13 December; the next day the fever broke. As his mother said, the Prince had been brought back from 'the very verge of the grave'. Once he had regained full health, the government, sensing a changed mood among the people, was quick to suggest that there should be a public thanksgiving for the Prince's recovery. The celebrations, which climaxed with a special service in St Paul's Cathedral, was, as Gladstone recorded, a quite 'extraordinary manifestation of loyalty and affection'. The royal carriage – an open landau drawn by six gleaming horses – was cheered by the dense crowds lining the route. 'It was a most affecting day', the Queen noted in her journal.

Down at the Crystal Palace – now well established in its second home in Sydenham, south London – a choir of more than 2,000 singers and a massive orchestra, which included a military band, were assembled for the premiere of a *Te Deum* specially composed by Sir Arthur Sullivan. Some 30,000 attended the concert, including Princess Louise (one of Edward's sisters), the Duke of Edinburgh (one of his brothers), the Prince and Princess of Teck, and the Duke of Cambridge, the Queen's first cousin and the army's commander in chief.

The following year, an abortive attempt on the Queen's life by a 17-year-old Irish youth called Arthur O'Connor provoked even more of a reaction in her favour. The tactless Dilke tried to return to the question of the Queen's finances in the House of Commons, but he was howled down. When he also attempted to criticise the monarchy in a speech at Bolton, his words were drowned out by the crowd singing 'Rule Britannia' and 'God Save the Queen.' It seemed that the nation's feelings towards the Queen and her family had been transformed.

HIGH DAYS AND HOLIDAYS

Preoccupied as he was with Ireland and what he termed 'a great crisis of Royalty', Gladstone had little time to take much personal interest in the other reforming measures that his administration was busily passing into law. Some of these, though, probably had a greater and more lasting effect on the country's way of life than did his tinkering with the Irish Question.

In 1871, the Bank Holiday Act became law. It was sorely needed. The Factory and Workshops Act of 1867 had stipulated that people should not work for longer than 60 hours a week, but the types of workers who benefited from its provisions

continued on page 52

MR AND MRS BROWN
Queen Victoria seated in her pony chaise, with some of her grandchildren around her, in the garden of Osborne House on the Isle of Wight. Her personal attendant and ghillie John Brown stands at the pony's head. Victoria and Brown became such close friends that their relationship caused scandal throughout the court and government of the time. The 'great court favourite,' as he was referred to by the *John O'Groats Journal*, was certainly indulged by the Queen at every opportunity. Lord Stanley commented that she was 'really doing all in her power to create suspicions … everything shows that she had selected this man for the kind of friendship that is unwise and unbecoming in her position.' The Queen was impervious to criticism. In her *Leaves from the Journal of Our Life in the Highlands* she described Brown as possessing 'all the independence and elevated feelings peculiar to the Highland race'. For his part, Brown helped the Queen to overcome her grief. He served her devotedly for 34 years before he died at Windsor in 1883.

A RAILWAY FOR WORK AND PLAY

The Ffestiniog Mountain Railway had been founded as far back as 1832 to serve the slate quarries of Blaenau Ffestiniog. It was a narrow-gauge line, powered by horses for many years, who hauled empty wagons from Porthmadog on the coast up to the slate quarries. Once loaded, the wagons made the return journey down the gradient on their own, powered by the force of gravity. The line was converted to steam power in 1863, using specially commissioned small locomotives. The following year the line was granted permission to run passenger trains, the first narrow-gauge railway in Britain to do so.

But the small locomotives could only pull small trains. An important breakthrough came in 1870 when a pioneer double-bogie engine, designed by engineer Robert Fairlie, made its debut. To the layman, it looked like two locomotives joined back to back. It doubled the power of the previous engines, enabling longer trains to run on the line and blazing a trail for narrow-gauge railways all over the world. The line began to attract another type of customer, who would become increasingly important as time went on – holidaymakers drawn by the wild beauty of Snowdonia. The line still runs today, thanks to the efforts of steam railway enthusiasts. The photograph shows a passenger train (far left) making way for a descending passenger-cum-goods train going through Tan-y-Bwlch, one of the stations along the line.

were limited. Many remained unprotected. Bank clerks, for instance, were often expected to start at 8.30 in the morning and remain at their desks until nine or ten at night. Paid overtime was unheard of, while any time at work spent not actually working – eating lunch, for instance – was unpaid. There was no such thing as paid holiday. The Bank Holiday Act pioneered the notion of holidays with pay by creating four official public holidays – on Boxing Day, Easter Monday, Whit Monday and the first Monday in August in England and Wales (arrangements for Scotland were slightly different).

Time for cricket

The Act was piloted through the House of Commons by Sir John Lubbock, a Liberal backbencher who, as well as being a prominent banker, was a noted amateur archaeologist, botanist and cricket enthusiast. It was his love of cricket that led him to press for the legislation. Lubbock felt strongly that his bank clerks should have the chance to participate in village cricket matches, but he did not see why his competitors should gain a commercial advantage over him by keeping their banks open while his were closed.

Cricket was rapidly emerging as the favourite sport of the Victorian middle classes. The County Championship was established in 1873 and the first national Australian team arrived to tour the mother country five years later. By the end of the decade it was not uncommon to see crowds of up to 10,000 at county

SPORTING HEROES
The handsomely bearded Dr W G Grace (above), seated at the centre of the England team that would take on the Australians (right) in 1878. It was the first tour by a white all-Australian side, although an Aboriginal cricket team had visited a decade earlier and played up and down the country. The first test matches between the two countries were played two years later. Grace would be one of the stalwarts of the British cricketing scene from 1870 until his final retirement in 1910.

Many of the players, including Grace himself, were amateurs, though some professionals were employed, most often as bowlers. Class distinction between the two groups of 'Gentlemen' and 'Players' meant that the latter were often treated little better than serfs. The two entered cricket grounds by different gates, dressed in different pavilions and even travelled to matches in different train compartments.

matches, as people flocked to watch and marvel at the exploits of the sport's new superstars, such as ace batsman Dr W G Grace. Though notionally an amateur – he was a doctor by profession – it is estimated that Grace earned no less than £120,000 from his cricketing career, a huge sum at the time. Football, horse racing and the new sport of lawn tennis were all gaining or maintaining their popularity. For tennis, gentlemen wore knickerbockers and long black stockings, while ladies tied their skirts back to make it easier to run about the court. They wore aprons with pockets over their skirts to hold the spare balls.

The Bank Holiday Act also promoted the seaside day-tripper phenomenon. Brighton, for instance, boomed. Easy access from the capital won it the nickname 'London by the Sea.' Particularly on the August Bank Holiday, thousands of trippers poured off the trains and into the town to sample its delights. Visitors were serenaded by street singers, entertained by organ grinders and snapped by itinerant photographers. They were invited to partake of fruit, sweets, gingerbread, shellfish or ice cream, and urged to give a penny or two to a puppet or performing animal show. It was, said one observer, 'pandemonium on the sands.' Brighton's greatest rival in the south-east was Southend-on-Sea, which drew visitors primarily from the East End. Up in Lancashire, Blackpool, with its celebrated 'Golden Mile,' emerged as the north's foremost seaside resort.

continued on page 64

BESIDE THE SEA

Day-trippers and other holiday-makers promenade at Southend-on-Sea, one of the thriving seaside resorts that sprang up along Britain's coasts in Victorian times. It was all made possible by the coming of the railways. Before then, the seaside was the fashionable haunt of a select few rather than the general masses.

Bournemouth, for instance, was almost entirely a railway creation. As late as 1841 it was a village with fewer than 30 buildings, but when the railway finally reached the town in 1870, it triggered an immediate and rapid expansion. For a time Brighton attempted to preserve its exclusivity, but it finally gave way to the irresistible pressure as thousands of Londoners poured off the London to Brighton line. By contrast, Skegness on the coast of Lincolnshire was already a town of some substance and it practically begged the railway to come. The result was a golden age of unparalleled seaside prosperity.

What eventually emerged was a hierarchy of resorts, whose rankings depended on how easy it was to get there and how much it cost. Margate in Kent, for example, was inexpensive and so the natural destination for the lower middle classes, as was nearby Ramsgate, where the Chatham and Dover railway terminus was practically on the beach. Broadstairs was harder and more expensive to get to, so it attracted the more socially select. Blackpool in Lancashire was solidly working class, catering for workers on a hard-earned break from their labours in the burgeoning cotton mills. Southend itself became the holiday home of London's East Enders.

STREET TRADE

Victorian streets bustled with traders. Sellers included butchers' boys calling for orders and returning with trays of meat held high on the shoulder, while potmen carried jugs of porter and stout. Buyers included rag and bone men and scrap-metal dealers. There were repairers and service providers, such as knife grinders, lamplighters and chimney sweeps. In 1877 John Thomson and Adolphe Smith published a collection of photographs of these traders in *Street Life in London*, a selection of which are shown here.

SELLING BY SEASON
A fruit seller (below) peddles strawberries from a cart with the cry 'strawberries, all ripe'. Lavender girls and flower sellers would call 'all a-growing, all a-blowing.' In winter, there were sellers of sawdust-stuffed draught excluders, roasted chestnuts and baked potatoes. The muffin man, with his bell and a tray on his head, was a teatime fixture at any time of year.

BARROW BARGAINS
A fancy-wear dealer (right) displays his latest china ornaments for sale. The fancy-wear goods that found the readiest market were small personal items, such as combs for holding back hair, ear drops, finger rings, scarf pins, brooches and bracelets. Other traders offered everything ranging from toys and puzzles to toasting forks. There were animal sellers – rats, mice and squirrels were all firm favourites, along with songbirds and hedgehogs, which were useful for keeping down black beetles in the home. Health care was also for sale: street dentists and quack doctors, both armed with a battery of wonder cures, did a roaring trade.

'No city that I have ever visited will compare with London for the number of its street peddlers, hawkers, booth proprietors, open-air performers, ballad singers, mountebanks [acrobats] and other street itinerants.'

Daniel Kirwan, *American traveller*

SELLING THEIR WARES
Bill-stickers paste posters advertising the latest attractions at Madame Tussaud's waxwork museum (above left), while a sandwich-board man paces the street (centre). Popularly known as 'ladder-men', bill-stickers worked from 7.00am to 7.00pm, earning between £1 and £1 15s a week. According to Dickens, any empty shop front would be 'brought down to the condition of old cheese' by thick layers of 'rotting paste and rotting paper'. Menders, such as this locksmith (above right), relied on physical presence and word of mouth to find trade.

FLOWERS AND SHELLFISH
Flower girls sell bouquets in Covent Garden (far left), while customers line up at a shellfish stall to buy oysters, whelks, cockles and mussels. Flowers came up fresh from the country and went on sale in the early morning; shellfish stalls were usually outside pubs and did their best business in the early afternoon. Other street food sellers included piemen, who sold cakes and sweetmeats, and vendors of fried fish, kidney puddings and sheep's trotters. Drinks on offer included stout, porter, ginger beer, elder wine, and hot tea and coffee.

TAKING THE AIR

An umbrella mender takes a break to buy some ginger beer (left), while two costermongers pose with their donkey (below). Ginger beer was a popular street beverage; according to one estimate, around 300,000 gallons were sold each year in London alone. It was an easy trade to get into, for, as the compilers of *Street Life in London* recorded, it required 'little capital, no skill and scarcely any knowledge'. Often, the biggest problem was finding a receptacle large enough to hold the water in which the ginger was boiled, which was why many resorted to the 'disgusting habit of boiling ginger in the same vessel which serves for washing the dirty linen of several families'.

Costermongers were the cream of the street traders, selling fruit, vegetables and fish from stalls, barrows or occasionally a donkey and cart. On average, it is reckoned that they made between £1 and £5 a week, though as one observer put it, their 'harum-scarum, reckless, random, happy-go-lucky' characters meant that earnings ranged from 'quite large sums of money to almost nothing at all'. The dapper young man leaning against the rail was the son of the owner of one of two stables that sold donkey rides on Clapham Common during the season. On good days, the donkey-ride business could bring in between £1 and £1 10s.

Becoming a shoe-black was one way that a boy could make a living (right), but it was not that easy to take it up. Independent shoe-blacks had to face the hostility of the so-called Boot-blacking Brigade and harassment by police on the beat. It also cost 5 shillings to get the necessary licence.

STREET CONCERT

A young Italian harpist plays in the street, entertaining both children and adults in the hope of earning a few pennies. The harp, being quite bulky, was an unusual instrument for a busker. This one seems to be going down quite well, but that was not always the case. Many Victorians regarded buskers as public nuisances and groaned inwardly at the sound of an approaching barrel organ, hurdy-gurdy or piano organ. There were also so-called German bands, which, according to W S Gilbert in *Princess Ida*, made a habit of 'playing Wagner incorrectly'.

PERSONAL SOUVENIR

A young family pose for a photograph on Clapham Common, keen to have a permanent memento of their day out. As well as technical skill, itinerant photographers needed the gift of the gab to attract passing trade, but their services grew increasingly popular with day-trippers. Children's nannies were another favourite target. 'The photographer', it was noted in *Street Life in London*, 'can generally rely on receiving more orders once he has secured the custom of a nurse-girl.'

There was also a darker side to the photographic success story. Pornographic images were widely offered for sale by mail order or behind closed doors. In 1874 police raided two studios in Pimlico owned by Henry Hayler and seized no fewer than 130,000 obscene photographs. Hayler fled the country, ending up in Berlin, though history does not record whether he set up a new business there.

CONTROVERSIAL MEASURES

DEEP CLEAN
Two public disinfectors with their cart outside a shed housing a disinfecting oven. The job of public disinfector was created as a result of public health reforms instituted in the 1870s to deal with outbreaks of smallpox and other contagious diseases. The ovens were used to fumigate clothes, bedding, curtains and carpets collected from the homes of victims. Working in conjunction with public health inspectors – known as 'inspectors of nuisances' at the time – the disinfectors stripped homes of everything that might harbour infection. Then they sealed the sickroom airtight and burned sulphur in it for 24 hours. After that, wallpaper was stripped off and the room washed down with carbolic acid.

There seemed no limit to the administration's reforming zeal. The Married Woman's Property Act allowed married women to keep £200 of their own money, rather than having to hand every penny over to their husbands. In the teeth of fierce opposition from landlords and employers, the Ballot Act made secret voting compulsory, so reducing the risk of election results being corrupted by bribery or coercion. The Public Health Act divided the country into Health Authority districts, each with its own Medical Officer of Health, while the Trade Union Act gave the newly emerging trade unions legal status and legalised the right to strike.

In this last instance, what the reformers gave with one hand, they took away with the other, for the Criminal Law Amendment Act made all forms of picketing during an industrial dispute illegal. This lost the Liberal government much working class support, especially after the conviction of five London gas stokers for conspiracy in 1871. The stokers had formed a union to press for more pay, fewer hours – they were expected to work 80 hours a week – and Sunday off. Though 14 out of the 25 gas works in the capital agreed to the demands, the giant Beckton works, owned by the Gas, Light & Coke Company, dismissed the men it believed to be behind the demands. The stokers promptly went on strike to try to force the company to reinstate their colleagues.

In all, some 2,000 stokers downed tools, but the strike was quickly broken. The London correspondent of the *New York Times* was quick to applaud the Gas, Light & Coke Company's decision to sack the strikers out of hand and prosecute their leaders. After describing for his readers how 'when on Monday, the gas began to flicker and grow faint, and sometimes to die away altogether, people were terribly afraid the whole town would be plunged into darkness', he went on to assert that the strikers had little public support and 'were repeatedly hissed and groaned at along the way' as they marched to Trafalgar Square. The article concluded: 'It is certainly time to make working men understand that they cannot play fast and loose with engagements as they please, and that there are other laws beside the edicts of the trade unions.' Sir William Brett, the presiding judge in the case, concurred. He chose to ignore the jury's recommendation for mercy, and sentenced each of the defendants to imprisonment for a year.

MEDICAL MATTERS

St Thomas's Hospital in its new buildings completed in 1871 on a site in Lambeth, viewed from across Westminster Bridge, which had opened just a decade earlier. St Thomas's was one of Victorian London's leading teaching hospitals. It was there that Florence Nightingale founded the world's first professional school of nursing. Many doctors had a thin time of it in the 1870s. Physicians and surgeons at the top of their profession could command large fees, but the majority worked hard to scrape a living. Many folk preferred to rely on patent panaceas. The original Beecham's Pills promised to cure everything from scurvy to bad dreams. In fact, they contained only aloes (a purgative), ginger and soap.

A LUCKY FEW
Pupils at Christ's Hospital School pictured with masters outside the old school buildings in the heart of the City of London (above). The school had been founded by Edward VI in 1552.

EDUCATING THE POOR
Lord Shaftesbury (left) with a young pupil at one of the capital's Ragged Schools for destitute children. Shaftesbury was one of Victorian Britain's leading social reformers and philanthropists, presiding over the Ragged Schools Union for over 30 years. The first Ragged School had been established in Aberdeen in 1841. By the time the 1870 Education Act became law, 350 of them had been set up around the country. It is estimated that they provided 300,000 destitute children with an elementary education. After the passing of the Education Act, the Ragged Schools were gradually absorbed into the new Board Schools established under the Act.

Teaching the children

The Education Act that the Liberals passed in 1870 proved just as controversial. There was little doubt that the subject was of growing concern. According to one commentator, 'the rising generation' were 'growing up in ignorance, wickedness and forgetfulness of God'. Setting up better schools and improving existing ones would, it was felt, ensure that Britain's children were educated 'in God's fear, in knowledge of His ways and in the daily remembrance of His commandments.'

It was hardly surprising that religion figured so strongly in Victorian educational thinking. Before 1870, the churches had run the majority of what were termed National Schools, which taught young children the basics of reading, writing and arithmetic. Attendance was voluntary and, in any event, the number of schools was totally inadequate. Then there were the so-called Ragged Schools, set up by philanthropists such as Lord Shaftesbury to provide education for the poorest children among the burgeoning population. William Locke, the secretary of the London Ragged School Union, summed up the nature of the 13,000 children in his schools: 'Many of them are homeless; many of them are entirely neglected by their parents; many are orphans, outcasts, street beggars, crossing sweepers and little hawkers of things about the streets; they are generally very ignorant, although in some points very quick and cunning.'

William Edward Forster, a Quaker philanthropist and Vice-President of the Council with responsibility in Cabinet for education, was quick to call for action. 'On the speedy provision of elementary education', he warned the House of Commons, 'depends our industrial prosperity, the safe working of our constitutional system and our national power. Civilised communities throughout the world are massing themselves together, each mass being measured by its force: and if we are to hold our position among men of our own race or among the nations of the world, we must make up the smallness of our numbers by increasing the intellectual force of the individual.'

Forster's Bill divided England and Wales into some 2,500 school districts, each with its own School Board elected by the ratepayers. In a historic first for Britain, women were allowed to vote for the Boards and to stand for election. Elizabeth Garrett Anderson, a popular local doctor, put her name forward as a candidate in Marylebone and topped the poll with 47,000 votes – more than any other candidate in the country. The boards were charged with examining existing school provision in their respective districts, and if there were not enough places, they could then build and maintain new schools to be paid for out of the rates.

Building Board Schools

The Act certainly brought about much-needed change. Before it, 40 Birmingham children out of every hundred were running loose in the streets. In Manchester, the figure was 50 out of a hundred. In London, 455,000 children were in need of elementary education; if every child of primary school age was taken into account the capital was short of 100,000 school places. It was estimated that a staggering 176,000 children in London were receiving no education at all.

Faced with this shortfall, which was particularly serious in the East End, the London School Board took emergency action. Temporary schools were set up under railway arches and in basements under workshops until new schools could be built. The Old Castle Street Board School in Whitechapel was the first to be completed, in 1873. By April 1875, it had been joined by 53 more, providing places for 50,000 children. The least efficient Ragged and Voluntary Schools were taken over and grants allocated to the best of them to help them to reach Board School standards.

'Some believe the first government of Mr Gladstone in its dealing with education to have achieved its greatest constructive work. Others think that, on the contrary, it threw away a noble chance.'

John Morley

Such improvements were not confined to the capital. The Labour politician Philip Snowden recalled in his autobiography how the school he attended as a boy of 10 to 11 in the West Riding of Yorkshire was taken over by a newly formed School Board. 'Steps were taken at once to build new premises and a trained master was appointed', he wrote. 'We were taught in a new schoolroom, which, by comparison with the dingy place we left seemed a palace to us.'

So why was the Education Act so controversial? The answer boiled down to one simple caue – religion, and a bitter dispute about whether religious instruction should be provided in the new schools. Church of England traditionalists, banded together in the National Education Union, wanted the denominational system to continue, while the National Educational League, founded in Birmingham by Joseph Chamberlain and others and widely supported by Nonconformists, favoured a secular option. The government sat uneasily on the fence between the two. The historian G M Young succinctly summed up the situation. 'No party would have dared to turn the Bible out of the schools, and no two parties could agree as to the terms upon which it should be admitted.' The compromise the government eventually devised ended up pleasing no one.

The Act had other failings, too. Though the intention was to provide an education for all children between 5 and 13 years of age, it did not make school attendance compulsory. That had to wait another decade. Nor was the schooling necessarily free. Places at the new Board Schools had to be paid for, unless parents could show that they were too poor to pay. The Act did not even attempt to touch on secondary education, which remained an upper and middle-class preserve. As to the kind of technical education that an enlightened Germany was already providing for thousands of students, nothing remotely like it would be attempted in Britain until the 20th century.

SOLDIERS OF THE QUEEN
Recruiting sergeants from three of the army's crack cavalry regiments lounge outside the Mitre and Dove tavern on the corner of King Street and Bridge Street, Westminster, keeping a watchful eye out for potential recruits (top right). Sergeant Walls of the 1st Battalion Grenadier Guards poses in full-dress uniform, complete with regimental bearskin (right). Despite much needed army reforms brought in by Edward Cardwell, Secretary of State for War, many serving soldiers found military life too hard to bear. 'Our soldiers', the compilers of *Street Life in London* recorded, 'run away at the rate of more than 21 a day.' In 1876, there were no fewer than 7,759 deserters on the run.

Reforming the army

Curiously enough for a government whose election-winning slogan had been 'Peace, Retrenchment and Reform', the Liberals spent substantial amount of parliamentary time reforming the armed forces. This was never meant to dominate their agenda in the way that it did, but against the background of the Franco-Prussian War, Gladstone and his colleagues felt compelled to review the nation's military resources.

Under the terms of the Treaty of London, signed in 1839, Britain was committed to defend the independence of Belgium. People might chuckle initially at the appearance of an advertisement in *The Times* for toy 'Prussian Pop-Guns. Rare Fun', but they became seriously alarmed when Edward Cardwell, the Secretary of State for War, was compelled to admit to the House of Commons that he was not sure that the army was in a position to find the 20,000 men it was calculated would be needed should Belgian neutrality be violated. The response was just what Cardwell wanted. The press began an immediate clamour for army reform. Cardwell was determined to drag the army into modern times by abolishing the system of officers purchasing commissions and doing away with such practices as flogging and branding. In Cardwell's reformed army, officers would be

'British officers were expected to be gentlemen and sportsmen, but outside the barrack yard they were entirely wanting in military knowledge. The lack of it was deemed no drawback since Marlborough's and Wellington's officers got along without it.'

R C K Ensor, historian

selected on merit, rather than because they could afford to buy their positions, and the soldiers they commanded would be treated more humanely. The War Office was reorganised and the terms of enlistment altered. Partly as an economy measure but also to attract more recruits, soldiers could now enlist for shorter periods – usually six years with the colours and six in reserve. Finally, the regimental system was reorganised on the basis of two linked battalions, one serving overseas while the other stayed at home.

Needless to say, nearly every senior army officer from the Duke of Cambridge, the commander in chief, downwards opposed Cardwell's reforms. 'Changes are always bad,' complained one. Following in their footsteps, diehard former military men in the House of Commons – the 'colonels' as they became known – used every trick in the book to hold up the legislation. So bitter was the House of Lords opposition to the abolition of purchase that eventually Gladstone persuaded the Queen to end it by revoking the Royal Warrant that her grandfather, George III, had used to sanction it in the first place. Parliamentary purists tut-tutted at the way Parliament had been bypassed, but Gladstone was delighted. At a cost of £8 million paid out to officers who suffered from the measure, the reform was law.

'EXHAUSTED VOLCANOES'

By 1872, Gladstone's government was running out of steam – as was the man himself. Disraeli recognised that the time had come to attack. On 3 April, 1872, speaking at the Free Trade Hall, Manchester, he denounced Gladstone, his government and all its works in a mammoth speech lasting three-and-a-half hours. He was fortified throughout by the mounting cheers of his audience and, so Henry Cecil Raikes, Conservative MP for Chester, reported, the consumption of two bottles of white brandy.

Disraeli's words were to resonate around the entire country. Gladstone, he said, was a treacherous Radical wolf disguised in a moderate's clothing. As for the administration, he declared scornfully that it reminded him of 'one of those marine landscapes not very unusual on the coasts of South America. You behold a range of exhausted volcanoes. Not a flame flickers on a single pallid crest. But the situation is still dangerous. There are occasional earthquakes and ever and anon the dark rumbling of the sea.' At the Crystal Palace in June, speaking in searing heat, Disraeli launched a blistering attack on Liberalism, which, he said, 'is viewed by the country with disgust'. On contrast, the Conservatives would 'elevate the condition of the people' and 'uphold the Empire'.

It seemed that almost everything the Liberals touched now served only to worsen their political fortunes and increase their unpopularity. Their Licensing Act was a case in point. Introduced in response to sustained pressure from supporters of the temperance movement – the most influential pressure group was the United Kingdom Alliance – it alienated drinkers across the land. The first bill was so

RESTRICTING THE DEMON DRINK

Two ageing country labourers enjoy a pint in a village outside Stratford-on-Avon (right). In the 1870s, drinking was a national pastime. There were pubs in abundance – on busy London streets, it was not uncommon to find one every 100 yards. Edinburgh had a pub for every 30 families, Dundee one for every 24. Even in the supposedly hard-working City of London, it was the custom, noted R D Blumenfeld, for 'businessmen of all ranks to knock off at eleven o'clock in the morning for a drink, champagne at 6d a glass being the favourite tipple'.

Most pubs were drab and modest. A typical pub in York consisted of a shabby bar parlour with room for just 10 drinkers at a time. But despite there being 13 other pubs within five minutes' walk, on a typical day it still served 550 customers, of whom 258 were men and the remainder women. For the working classes, pubs were social centres, which was why all attempts to restrict opening hours led to fierce protests. At one time, it was estimated that 70 per cent of working men in Derby spent their entire evenings in pubs. Some working-class families were spending more than half their earnings on drink.

Gladstone's Licensing Act did little but cause resentment. Disraeli's Act, which was passed soon after his return to power, was more acceptable. Pubs outside the capital had to close by midnight. London pubs were allowed to open on weekdays from 5.00 in the morning until 12.30 at night, but had to close at midnight on Saturday. Sunday opening was the most restricted, with pubs allowed to open from 1.00 to 3.00 in the afternoon and 6.00 to 11.00 in the evening. The hours remained unchanged until after the outbreak of the First World War in 1914.

savaged it had to be withdrawn and a second measure hastily substituted. But even this watered-version led to the outbreak of sporadic riots. Many ordinary folk believed it was clear evidence the Liberals thought that there should be one law for the rich, free to drink at home and in their clubs, and another for the poor.

For the first time, limits were placed on the sale of alcohol. Vendors had to apply for a licence from the local magistrates, who could also decide on opening hours. Brewers and publicans were incensed by what they saw as a curb on their freedom, while the Tories seized the opportunity to put themselves forward as the champions of the beer-drinking working man. It was a brave – or foolhardy – government that dared to come between the working man and his pint.

Gladstone's fall

As Liberal splits increased and the government's unpopularity grew, the end, it seemed, was approaching fast, but in the event it did not come quickly. It looked as though Gladstone's time was up when his Irish Universities Bill, which he had made an issue of confidence, was thrown out by three votes. He resigned, recommending to the Queen that she send for Disraeli. But the canny Conservative leader, mindful of how hard he had found it to lead a minority administration, refused to form a government. Gladstone was forced to resume office, with much diminished prestige. Matters worsened as financial irregularities in the Post Office came to light. William Monsell, the Postmaster General, resigned and Robert Lowe, the Chancellor of the Exchequer, was abruptly shifted to the Home Office. Gladstone took on the added burden of the Exchequer. Soon, believing that his government had been reduced to impotence, he asked the Queen to dissolve Parliament.

The General Election of February 1874 gave the Tories an overall majority of more than 50 seats. Gladstone put most of the blame for his defeat on the brewers, telling his brother that he had been 'borne down in a torrent of gin and beer'. In truth, the country had grown tired of him and his ministry. Not even his pledge to abolish income tax could win back the voters. The Queen was convinced that his defeat 'was greatly owing to his own unpopularity and to the want of confidence people had in him'. One member of the Liberal Cabinet put it rather differently. 'We had exhausted our programme & quiet men asked what will Gladstone do next? Will he not seek to recover his popularity by extreme radical measures?'

Gladstone's first administration was over. Since he was now 65 years old, it would have been reasonable to suppose that it would be his last. With Disraeli at the helm, the country looked forward to a new, Conservative future.

IMPERIAL
ECHOES

When Disraeli became Prime Minister in 1874, it was the second time that he had climbed to the 'top of the greasy pole'. In the General Election, he had trounced Gladstone and the Liberals, winning outright victory for the Conservatives for the first time in more than 30 years. Now, at the age of 70, he formed his second administration.

DEFENDERS OF THE RAJ Major-General Sir Frederick Roberts, later Lord Roberts, with Indian officers in the service of the British Raj.

DISRAELI'S DAY

At home, Disraeli promised to 'improve the condition of the people'. Abroad he pledged to show 'a little more energy in foreign affairs' than had his predecessor. Though he would have liked his country to be more influential in Europe, circumstances limited Britain to a peripheral role. Imperially, though, was quite a different matter. In November 1875, Disraeli pulled off one of the coups of his career. He purchased for Britain the bankrupt Khedive of Egypt's shares in the Suez Canal. It was the start of a romantic odyssey that climaxed with the Queen's proclamation as Empress of India.

Gladstone's record

Gladstone's foreign policy had been far less successful than his domestic one. He made a vigorous attempt to persuade Bismarck not to annex Alsace-Lorraine from defeated France after the Franco-Prussian War. But Bismarck was not to be moved, refusing to be lectured on political morality by the man he contemptuously christened 'Professor Gladstone'. In the long term, Gladstone was proved right. He told the Queen – 'in a very excited manner', she noted – that there would 'never be a cordial understanding with Germany if she took that million and a quarter people against their will.'

Gladstone continued to moralise, but was powerless to act. He appeared equally ineffectual when Russia took advantage of the Franco-Prussian conflict to denounce the treaty that had ended the Crimean War a decade earlier and closed the Black Sea to its warships. His rather lame response was to summon an international conference, which tried to save face by legalising the action after the event, declaring that treaties could not be abrogated unilaterally, but needed the consent of all their signatories. Finally,

continued on page 78

'If you look back to the history of this country since the advent of Liberalism forty years ago, you will find that there has been no effort as continuous ... as the attempts of Liberalism to effect the disintegration of the Empire ...'

Benjamin Disraeli

WAITING IN THE WINGS

Disraeli in 1872 (left), the year his beloved wife died. He is captured deep in contemplation of a book, possibly one of his own novels. Disraeli disliked most of his fellow authors. He never forgave Thackeray for cruelly lampooning him, or Trollope for referring to him in public as 'a conjuror and a charlatan'. At the time this photograph was taken, Disraeli was watching from the opposition benches as Gladstone's Liberal administration began to run out of steam. Yet when the Conservative victory came, in February 1874, the size of the majority took Disraeli somewhat by surprise. It was the first time the Conservatives had won an outright majority of seats since 1841. *Punch* portrayed him soaring aloft on the wings of victory (right). Gladstone was stung by the public rejection of him and his government. Shortly afterwards, he resigned from the leadership of the Liberal Party

PARADISE AND THE PERI.

COUNTRY RETREAT

Disraeli (standing left) is pictured below in 1874 with friends in the gardens of Hughenden Manor, his Buckinghamshire country home. Standing alongside is Lord Pembroke (centre) and Lord Wharncliffe; seated is Selina, Countess of Bradford (left), Lady Susan Wharncliffe and Orlando Bridgeman, 3rd Earl of Bradford. Lying at the front is Montagu William Corry, Disraeli's private secretary. Disraeli conducted a passionate correspondence with Selina. Writing to her, he assured the Countess, 'was my duty and delight; the duty of my heart and the delight of my life'. When Disraeli, then Lord Beaconsfield, resigned as Prime Minister following his 1880 election defeat, he begged the Queen to make Corry a lord in the Dissolution Honours. The Queen obliged and Corry became 1st Baron Rowton. Gladstone joked that nothing like it had been seen since Caligula had made his horse a Consul.

78 *Passage de Prince de Gall*

THE LION'S SHARE.

THE WAY TO THE EAST

Carrying Edward, Prince of Wales, to India in October 1875, the specially converted troopship *Seraphis* enters the Suez Canal at Port Said, escorted by a Royal Navy frigate, with the royal yacht *Osborne* in attendance (left). By the time the Prince returned the following year, the canal would be jointly owned by Britain.

The Suez Canal had been masterminded by the French engineer Ferdinand de Lesseps and built as a French-Egyptian project. Within just a few years of its completion in 1869, the spendthrift Khedive of Egypt, Ismail Pasha, was struggling to avoid bankruptcy and Disraeli audaciously seized the chance to buy his shares in the Suez Canal Company – almost half of the total. This secured for Britain a controlling stake in the fastest route to India and the East. In the *Punch* cartoon (above), by John Tenniel, Disraeli is shown paying off the Khedive, while the British lion holds the key to India firmly between its paws.

RICH AS CROESUS
Lord Rothschild, head of the family merchant bank that bore his name, was one of the richest men in England. It was to Rothschild and his bank that Disraeli turned when he needed to borrow money quickly and discreetly to buy the Suez Canal shares. 'There was only one concern that could have done it', he told the Queen.

there was the *Alabama* settlement, by which Britain agreed to compensate the USA for the damage this Confederate privateer had done to Northern shipping during the American Civil War. With hindsight, this could be seen as the obvious course of action – Britain, after all, had at one stage been on the brink of recognising the Confederacy, and it was due to British negligence that the *Alabama* escaped detention in port. But at the time it was extremely unpopular. Alfred Tennyson told the Prime Minister quite bluntly that: 'If you let those Yankee sharpers get anything like their way in the *Alabama* claims, I won't pay my ship money any more than old Hampden.' Many shared Tennyson's view and looked back wistfully to the glory days of Palmerston with his gunboat diplomacy, blaming Gladstone and the Liberal government for these blows to British prestige.

Buying the Suez Canal

Disraeli's first great coup in foreign policy was largely accidental. It was sparked off by the worsening financial difficulties of Ismail Pasha, the playboy Khedive of Egypt, which forced him to put his holdings in the Suez Canal Company up for sale. It was scarcely surprising that the spendthrift Khedive was fast nearing bankruptcy. When the Prince of Wales had visited Egypt in 1869, the Egyptian ruler provided him with no fewer than six blue-and-gold steamers for his journey up the Nile. Each steamer towed a barge packed with provisions, including 3,000 bottles of champagne, 4,000 of claret and 20,000 of soda water. In a specially fitted-out palace in Alexandria lent to Edward for the occasion, he found his bedroom equipped with solid silver beds and chairs of beaten gold.

Who controlled the Suez Canal was a major strategic concern for Britain, as the waterway cut the time it took to sail to India by several weeks. By 1875, some 80 per cent of the canal's traffic was British. Even more importantly, if Russia ever attempted to invade India through Afghanistan, or in the event of another Indian Mutiny, reinforcements could reach the subcontinent far more speedily than if they had to take the more tortuous route around the Cape of Good Hope.

The Khedive was negotiating with two French banks – both of which were not only slow to respond but were also insisting on onerous terms – when Lionel de Rothschild, head of Britain's richest banking family, got wind of what was going

ROYAL ARRIVAL

Two giant model elephants and a welcoming party wait to greet the Prince of Wales on his arrival in Columbo, Ceylon (today's Sri Lanka) in December 1875. It was here that the Prince, a keen big-game hunter, shot his first elephant. He wrote home to his two young sons that he would bring a baby elephant back with him to Sandringham for them to ride.

Edward had begun his tour of India in Bombay (today's Mumbai) on 8 November, where he was welcomed by Sir Philip Wodehouse, Governor of the province, and Lord Northbrook, the Viceroy of India, who had travelled from Calcutta for the occasion. Hailed as the incarnation of the British Raj, the Prince was well received as he toured the subcontinent. His attitude towards his future subjects was universally

praised; indeed, he wrote to Lord Salisbury, Secretary of State for India, castigating the 'disgraceful' way in which some British officers referred to the Indians as 'niggers'. He wrote to Lord Granville, leader of the Liberals in the House of Lords in similar vein. 'Because a man has a black face and a different religion to our own', the Prince protested, 'there is no reason why he should be treated as a brute.'

on. He went straight to the Prime Minister, who recognised the potential immediately. Overriding opposition in his Cabinet, Disraeli decided on instant action. The problem was how to raise the hard cash the Khedive was demanding. Parliament was in recess, so no vote could be taken to raise funds, while it was illegal for the government to borrow money from the Bank of England.

Disraeli's answer was to raise a short-term loan from his friends, the Rothschilds. He sent his secretary, Montagu Corry, to call on Lionel de Rothschild at New Court, Lincoln's Inn, to request an immediate loan of £4 million. According to Corry, Rothschild was eating some grapes at this desk. Between mouthfuls, he asked two questions, 'How much?' and 'What is your security?', before spitting out a grape pip and saying laconically: 'You shall have them!' The bank charged the government a commission of 2.5 per cent and made £100,000 out of the transaction. The whole deal had taken less than 10 days from the time that Disraeli first heard the news. When Parliament reassembled, Sir Stafford Northcote, Chancellor of the Exchequer, paid off the loan by passing an Exchequer Bonds Bill, raising just over £4 million from the Post Office Savings Bank at 3.5 per cent and increasing income tax to 4d in the pound.

UPHOLDING THE RAJ

The Prince of Wales (centre), in solar topee, pictured outside Government House in Calcutta. Lord Northbrook, the Viceroy, is on the Prince's right, while to his left is Miss Emma Baring, the Viceroy's daughter. Prince Edward and the Viceroy got on well.

At the start of his visit, Edward hosted a Durbar in the throne room, receiving eight bejewelled Indian princes. A week of sightseeing, receptions, military reviews and visits to the races followed. His visit to Calcutta concluded with him unveiling a statue of Lord Minto, Northbrook's predecessor as Viceroy, who had been assassinated in 1872. He then watched a game of polo, before attending a state banquet and lavish farewell fireworks display. The evening's entertainment was rounded off with a performance of *My Awful Dad*, one of his favourite farces.

Though some, like Gladstone, grumbled, opinion in general was in favour of the purchase. Its sheer audacity captured the popular imagination. Disraeli declared triumphantly that 'the whole country is with me'. He told MPs that the people wanted 'the Empire to be maintained, to be strengthened; they will not be alarmed even if it is increased. Because they think we are obtaining a great hold and interest in this important portion of Africa, because they believe that it secures to us a highway to our Indian Empire and our other dependencies, the people of England have from the first recognised the propriety and wisdom of the step which we will sanction tonight.'

To the Queen, Disraeli wrote exultantly, 'It is just settled; you have it, Madam!' To his close friend Lady Bradford, he was even more euphoric, boasting 'We have had all the gamblers, capitalists and financiers of the world, organised and platooned in bands of plunderers against us ... and have baffled them all ... The Faery [Disraeli's pet nickname for the Queen] is in raptures.' And so she was. In her journal, Victoria noted that the purchase 'gives us complete security for India ... An immense thing,' while to Theodore Martin, biographer of the Prince Consort, she wrote: 'It is entirely the doing of Mr Disraeli, who has very large ideas and very lofty views of the position this country should hold.'

A visit to the 'Jewel in the Crown'

Even before the acquisition, Disraeli had been preoccupied with imperial affairs, largely as a consequence of the determination of the Prince of Wales to pay a state visit to India. Initially, the Queen was opposed to the whole idea, and Disraeli's main concern was where the money was to come from to pay for what he christened 'the Indian expedition'. 'He [the Prince] has not a shilling,' he wrote to Lord Salisbury, Secretary of State for India, after a visit to Windsor Castle in March 1875. 'She [the Queen] will not give him one. A Prince of Wales must not move in India in a mesquin manner. Everything must be done on an imperial scale etc., etc. This is what she said.' The Prince himself spoke to his 'creatures,' as Disraeli labelled his cronies, 'of spending, if necessary a million, and all that'.

Disraeli had to overcome much opposition to the visit, for many ordinary folk objected to the cost. *Reynolds Newspaper* said that working men were being robbed so that the Prince could enjoy himself. A crowd of 60,000 protested in Hyde Park and similar demonstrations took place around the country. Yet Disraeli persuaded Parliament to vote the necessary funds: £52,000 to the Admiralty for the transport of the Prince and his entourage, and £60,000 for the Prince's personal expenditure. The Indian government eventually chipped in a further £100,000. When the Prince voiced a complaint, Disraeli countered by telling him it was the government's apparent parsimony that had changed popular opinion.

The expedition left England on 11 October, 1875, and docked at Bombay on 8 November. It was not to return until the following March. The enthusiastic reception given the Prince on his arrival set the tone for the entire visit, which turned out to be a great success. Crowds cheered his progress all the way from the docks to Government House, many waving banners with effusive slogans, such as 'Tell Mama We're Happy' and 'Welcome To Our Future Emperor'.

Queen and Empress

The cheering crowds in India were more prescient than they could possibly have realised, for back home in Britain, the Queen was badgering Disraeli to declare her

RULERS OF THE RAJ

Members of the British Indian administration confer at Simla (above), summer capital of the Raj, under the chairmanship of Lord Northbrook, the Viceroy, seated third from the right. Northbrook chafed under London's control, because his view of the future of the British in India differed fundamentally from that of the government back in Britain. Northbrook believed that by implementing reforms and social improvements, the Raj could reconcile Indians to the continuance of British rule. But Lord Salisbury, mindful of the Indian Mutiny, was not convinced. 'One thing at least is clear', he wrote to Northbrook, 'no one believes in our good intentions. We are often told to secure ourselves by their affections, not by force. Our great-grandchildren may be privileged to do it, but not we.' He was even blunter to Sir Philip Wodehouse, the Governor of Bombay. 'India is held by the sword,' he stated, 'and its rulers must in all essentials be guided by the maxims which befit the government of the sword.'

Empress of India. She had been brooding on the matter ever since hosting Tsar Alexander II of Russia on his visit to Britain in 1874. The Tsar, as an emperor, outranked her and this rankled. Her mounting discontent was fuelled by her awareness that her eldest daughter Vicky, wife of the Crown Prince of Prussia, would also outrank her when Wilhelm became Kaiser, another emperor. In the Queen's eyes, this was a humiliation not to be borne.

Disraeli responded by introducing the Royal Titles Bill into Parliament. If it was passed, the Queen would become *Regina et Imperatrix* – Queen and Empress. Such was her excitement at the news that she agreed to open the 1876 session of Parliament in person. But largely because Disraeli failed to consult with the Opposition in advance of the announcement, it caused a Parliamentary storm. Even Lord Derby, the Foreign Secretary, admitted that the Bill was 'universally disliked', while Lord Hartington, who shared the Liberal leadership with Lord Granville following Gladstone's resignation, declared it 'inexpedient to impair the ancient and royal title of Sovereign by the addition of the designation Empress'. Lord Kimberley, former Colonial Secretary, was forthright. 'It is sad,' he stated, 'that the Queen is foolish enough to wish for the title of Empress, in order that her family may be put on an equality with the Continental Imperial Highnesses.' Gladstone denounced the proposal as 'a piece of tomfoolery'. Disraeli noted that throughout the debates Gladstone kept 'glancing looks at me that would have annihilated any man who had not a good majority and a determination to use it'.

Disraeli got his way and the Bill became law on 1 January, 1877. The Queen held a celebratory dinner at Windsor, though the countryside was so awash with

winter floods that her guests found it difficult to get through to the castle from London. The Queen astounded Disraeli and Lord George Hamilton, Undersecretary of State for India, by bedecking herself with ornate jewels, the gifts of Indian princes. Eventually, she would order the building of the Durbar Room at Osborne on the Isle of Wight to house her vast collection of Indian artefacts. It was the closest to the subcontinent she would ever get.

Celebrations in India were extravagant. Lord Lytton, recently appointed Viceroy, put Major-General Roberts in charge of preparations, instructing him to spare 'no trouble or expense … in making the ceremony altogether worthy of such a great historical event'. Potentates and princes assembled from all over India. 'Delhi', Roberts recorded, 'must have witnessed many splendid pageants when the Rajput, the Moghul and the Mahratta dynasties, each in its turn, was at the height of its glory; but never before had princes and chiefs of every race and creed come from all parts of Hindustan, vying with each other as to the magnificence of their entourage, and met together with the same objective, that of acknowledging and doing homage to one supreme ruler.' According to Roberts 'The ceremony was most imposing and in every way successful.' It was marred only by one unfortunate incident, when elephants which were assembled to lead the grand parade panicked at the firing of the royal salute and 'scampered off, dispersing the crowd in every direction.' Luckily, said Roberts 'there was no harm done beyond a severe shaking to their riders'.

continued on page 88

'The Faery is much excited about the doings at Delhi. They have produced great effect in India, and indeed throughout the world …'

Disraeli, on the proclamation of the Queen as Empress of India, 1877

EMPRESS OF INDIA
The Maharajah of Jodhpur (top right) was one of the influential Indian princes selected for presentation to the Prince of Wales during his stay in Calcutta. The Maharajahs of Gwalior, Jaipur, Kashmir, Patiala, Indore and the Begum of Bhopal were also presented. Shortly after the Prince's visit, the Queen – seen here in her imperial robes (right) – was proclaimed Empress of India on the steps of the Royal Exchange to a flourish of trumpets. Initially, the move was not universally popular – even some members of Disraeli's Cabinet objected, as well as leaders of the Liberal opposition. But the Queen was delighted and before long most Britons responded favourably. Victoria Arch, gateway to Peel Park in Salford (left), was erected to commemorate the proclamation.

POWER AND POMP IN INDIA

In India, the sahibs and their wives lived in a style that they could only have dreamed of at home. British engineers built thousands of miles of railways; the army garrisoned the fabled North-West Frontier; traders flourished from Bombay to Calcutta, as did tea planters in Ceylon and Assam; British officials ran all levels of the administration. As Lord Curzon would put it later, India was 'the biggest thing that the British are doing anywhere'.

RULING QUEEN
Women rulers, though not common, were by no means unknown. Shah Jehan (right), the Begum of Bhopal, was one of four successive female rulers of that state. She was presented to the Prince of Wales during his visit to Calcutta in 1875. He found her 'agreeably talkative'.

PROUD PRINCE
Maharajah Holkar of Indore (left) was an ally of the British, although his forebears had fought them. Princes ruled a third of the subcontinent and most appeared to be staunch upholders of the Raj. Lord Salisbury, however, was mistrustful. He warned the Viceroy that 'they will certainly cut every English throat they can lay hands on whenever they can do it safely'.

IN CONFERENCE
Sir George Campbell seated next to the Rajah of Sikkim at a meeting in Darjeeling in 1873. Campbell sponsored many reforms, including opening up the Bengali civil service to Indian entrants. Many opposed the move. Lord Salisbury wrote: 'I can imagine no more terrible future for India than that of being governed by competition-baboos.'

'The vast majority of Indians, I thoroughly believe, are well contented under our rule. They have changed masters so often, there is nothing humiliating to them in having gained a new one.'

Lord Salisbury, in a speech at the Royal Indian Engineering College, June 1873

WARRIORS

Officers (left) of the 72nd Highlanders outside their mess at Umballa in 1873. As much as a third of the British army was stationed in military camps and cantonments in India. As well as keeping order internally, the army kept a watchful eye on the turbulent North-West Frontier, frequently skirmishing with the border tribes who threatened the imperial peace.

PRINCES

Maharajahs (top) enjoyed all the trappings of office, but their actions were circumscribed. When the 12-year-old Gaekwar of Baroda presented six gold cannon, each worth £40,000, to the Prince of Wales, they were returned discreetly to his treasury. The idea was to let princes enjoy their accustomed grand status but not their former powers.

SPORTSMEN

Two polo teams (above) – one of British officers, the other of Indian nobles – before playing their first chukka in Hyderabad. The British adopted polo from the Indians, and in return introduced cricket to the subcontinent. Other pastimes included pig-sticking and big-game hunting. The Prince of Wales proved himself adept at both during his Indian visit.

TROUBLES AND TRIUMPHS

Disraeli had other foreign problems to face. 'Turkish affairs', said a member of the Cabinet, 'have taken hold of his mind and he can talk of nothing else.' In 1875 a peasant's revolt in Bosnia, then part of the Ottoman Empire, had sparked off a series of risings throughout the Balkans against Turkish rule. In April the next year, the Bulgarians revolted; during the following month, some 12,000 Bulgarian men, women and children were massacred by Turkish irregulars. Russia, self-proclaimed protector of the Slavs, stood poised to intervene.

In Britain, many people – notably in the industrial Midlands and the North – were appalled by reports of the slaughter. So, too, was Gladstone, who turned to his pen. In four days in late August, he compiled a pamphlet on the atrocities and what Britain's response to them should be, condemning the Turks as 'the one great anti-human species of humanity'. *The Bulgarian Horrors and the Question of the East* was published on 6 September and was an immediate hit. Mary Drew, Gladstone's daughter, recorded how 'Papa rushed off to London, pamphlet in hand, beyond anything agog over the Bulgarian horrors which pass description. The whole country is aflame – meetings all over the place.' In just three weeks, 200,000 copies of the pamphlet were sold.

'We don't want to fight, but …'

Disraeli was unmoved. Describing Gladstone's pamphlet as 'quite as unprincipled as usual though on the surface apparently not so ill-written as is his custom', he dismissed even the most gruesome tales of Ottoman barbarism, commenting that he believed the Turks 'seldom resort to torture, but generally expedite their connection with culprits in a more expeditious manner.' Having little sympathy with nationalist movements of any kind, he did not share the general feelings of outrage at Ottoman misrule. He was far more concerned about Russian intentions.

After the other great powers had failed in their diplomatic efforts to persuade the Ottoman regime to institute reforms, Russia declared war on Turkey in March 1877. Immediately, public opinion at home began to shift in the government's favour. Montagu Corry, Disraeli's private secretary, saw evidence of the change for himself when, shortly after the Russian-Turkish war broke out, he went 'to feel the pulse of the holiday-maker' at the London Pavilion, one of the capital's best-known music halls. 'There was one song, very badly sung,' Cory reported, 'but tumultuously cheered at the end of each verse'. The song was called 'Macdermott's War Song', after the music-hall star Gilbert Hastings Macdermott,

CONSTANTINOPLE CONFERENCE
At Disraeli's behest, Lord Salisbury (standing centre) took the lead at a conference called at Constantinople, in which the six great powers – Britain, France, Germany, Italy, Austria and Russia – attempted to pressure the Turks into introducing reforms designed to protect the Christian minorities in their tottering empire. Salisbury was not optimistic. He described his mission to his wife as 'an awful nuisance – not at all in my line – involving seasickness, much French and failure.' Much to the regret of Lord Derby, whom Salisbury was later to succeed as Foreign Secretary, Lady Salisbury accompanied her husband to the Turkish capital. 'She will certainly quarrel with the staff,' Derby predicted, 'and say and do the most imprudent things: having great cleverness, great energy and not a particle of tact.' On his arrival in Constantinople, following a whistle-stop tour of the major European capitals, Salisbury struck up a good relationship with Count Ignatiev (seated third from left), the Russian ambassador. But the Turks refused to be browbeaten into the reforms demanded at the conference.

PROPPING UP TURKEY

Seraglio Point (above), seen here from the far side of the Golden Horn, lay at the heart of Constantinople, capital of the decaying Ottoman Empire. The Tokapi Palace, Hagia Sophia and the Blue Mosque can all be clearly seen on the skyline. Regarded as 'the sick man of Europe' by all the other great powers, Turkey was facing the threat of Russian intervention to support the Slavs, who had revolted against continuing Ottoman tyranny in the Balkans.

For Disraeli, keeping Russia out of the Mediterranean was of primary British concern, so much so that he was prepared to go to war against the Tsar and in support of the Turks. But when the Russians attacked and drove the Turkish armies back on their capital, Disraeli found himself faced with a divided Cabinet. This did not stop him ordering the British fleet through the Dardanelles and into the Black Sea as a gesture of support for the Turks. The ships were cleared ready for action; here (right), gunners on HMS *Firefly* clean one of the deck guns.

otherwise known as the 'lion comique' or the Great Macdermott. The chorus brought down the house wherever and whenever it was sung, fuelling patriotic fervour as much as reflecting it:

> 'We don't want to fight, but by Jingo if we do,
> we've got the ships, we've got the men, and got the money, too.
> We've fought the Bear before, and while we're Britons true,
> the Russians shall not have Constantinople!' .

'Peace with honour'

Though his Cabinet was divided, Disraeli was quite prepared to go to war with Russia if Constantinople and what he considered to be vital British interests were threatened. Tension mounted as the Russians advanced on the Ottoman capital. With the enemy at the gates, the Turks sued for an armistice on 27 January. The Treaty of Stan Stefano gave Russia everything it wanted. As well as paying a huge indemnity, the Turks were forced to cede to the Tsar parts of Armenia, Georgia and the land between the lower River Danube and the Black Sea. They also had to recognise the independence of Romania, Serbia and Montenegro. Bulgaria grew vastly in size, and though not fully independent, it was given a Christian prince to rule it and allowed to raise an army of its own.

Although not directly involved, Disraeli was not prepared to accept the terms and nor, it seemed, were the British people. Major anti-Russian riots broke out. Gladstone found himself taunted by 'Jingoists' as he took his regular walk in Hyde Park. An angry mob stoned his London house in Harley Street, smashing windows and forcing him and his wife to take refuge with a neighbour. The Queen was even more anti-Russian than her subjects. Before long, she was threatening to 'lay down her crown' if the Cabinet compromised, rather than 'submit to Russian insult'.

To prop up the Turks, the fleet was ordered to sail through the Dardanelles to take up station in the Sea of Marmora. At home, the army reserve was called out, while units of the Indian Army prepared to sail for Malta, then on to Cyprus and Alexandretta on the southern Turkish coast. 'After all the sneers of our not having any great military force, the imagination of the Continent will be much affected by the first appearance of what they will believe to be an inexhaustible supply of men,' Disraeli explained to the Queen.

Gladstone described the provocation as 'intolerable' and denounced Disraeli for having committed 'an act of war, a breach of international law'. He was not alone. The novelist Henry James, now resident in London, wrote to an American friend: 'London smells of gunpowder and the tawdry old Jew who is at the head of this great old British Empire would like immensely to wind up his career with a fine long cannonade.' Fortunately, there were restraining influences at work. Lord Salisbury had succeeded Lord Derby as Foreign Secretary after the latter resigned in protest at sending in the fleet. He favoured negotiation, as did Austria-Hungary, itself alarmed at the prospect of Russian expansion in the Balkans. Bismarck, the Chancellor of Germany, put himself forward as what he termed an 'honest broker.' Russia was obliged to accept his offer and an international congress involving Britain, Russia, Austria-Hungary, Germany and France was held in Berlin that summer. No one thought it necessary to invite the defeated Turks.

Disraeli dominated proceedings from start to finish. Bismarck summed up his impact in one phrase – *Der alte Jude, das is der Mann* ('The old Jew, that's the man'). He returned to England in triumph, claiming that he was bringing with him 'peace with honour.' When the Channel ferry docked in Dover harbour, a vast crowd was on hand to greet him, singing along with the waiting band as it struck up 'Home, Sweet Home,' followed swiftly by 'Rule Britannia'.

The drive in an open barouche from Charing Cross station to Downing Street was even more momentous. The streets were packed with cheering people waving Union Jacks. In Downing Street, Sir Henry Ponsonby, the Queen's secretary, was waiting with a congratulatory letter and a bouquet of the premier's favourite flowers – a graceful tribute from a grateful sovereign. 'High and low are delighted', she later assured him, 'excepting Mr Gladstone, who is frantic.' The Queen offered Disraeli a dukedom, which he turned down, though he agreed to become a Knight of the Garter. He also accepted the freedom of the City of London. The celebrations were not confined to the capital. All over the country there was a brisk trade in commemorative plates, mugs and jars emblazoned with Disraeli's by now famous catchphrase. Some even bore depictions of the palace where the Congress took place.

Afghan imbroglio

As the government was soon to find, popular opinion could be as fickle as it was febrile. Two disasters in quick succession did major damage to the imperialist cause and gave Gladstone plenty of opportunity to trumpet his moral indignation at the course the country seemed to be taking. The first was in Afghanistan, which had been an almost constant thorn in the side of the British Raj in India since the

INTERVENTION IN AFGHANISTAN
Sir Louis Cavagnari, the prospective British representative in Afghanistan, sits cross-legged at the centre of a group of Afghan leaders as he attempted to negotiate with the border tribes to secure control of the Khyber Pass for Britain. It took a war to get him into Kabul, the Afghan capital, where he was appointed British Resident. Despite the assurances of the country's new Amir, Yakub Khan, Cavagnari and the other members of the British Legation were massacred by Afghan rebels on 3 September, 1879.

Britain reacted swiftly. The army – which had already invaded the country and forced Sher Ali, Yakub Khan's father, to flee to Turkestan – was ordered to occupy Kabul and Kandahar. Lord Salisbury, the Foreign Secretary, expressed the opinion that 'almost any severity' would be justified, from the wholesale razing of Kabul to the execution of every senior officer in the Afghan army.

SPOILS OF WAR

British commanders inspect rows of captured Afghan cannon (above) after Major-General Sir Frederick Roberts won a decisive victory at Kandahar. He and his troops had previously occupied Kabul (left), where they successfully withstood a 14-day siege. The war had been fought largely because Lord Lytton, the Viceroy of India, feared growing Russian influence in Afghanistan, which was seen as a prelude to Russia's occupation of the country. This, so Lytton believed, would directly threaten India itself. Though Disraeli's Cabinet warned him against any rash move, they reluctantly backed him once fighting had broken out. Gladstone fervently denounced 'this evil war.' When the Liberals were returned to power, he promptly ordered the country's evacuation.

time of the First Afghan War of 1839–42 in the days of the East India Company. Britain had worried ever since about the security of the north-west frontier, especially with the Russian Bear on the loose beyond. There had been fears of a Russian invasion of India via Afghanistan at the time of the Crimean War. Now Sher Ali, newly installed as his country's ruler, started to look to Russia to prop up his administration in the face of threatened rebellion

In July 1878, a Russian mission arrived in Kabul, the Afghan capital, while a British one was denied entry at the Afghan border. Lord Lytton responded from India with an ultimatum, demanding the Russian mission's withdrawal. When Sher Ali failed to respond, British and Indian troops under the command of Major-General Roberts poured through the Khyber Pass and advanced into the interior of Afghanistan.

Initially, the invasion was successful. Sher Ali fled his capital and in March 1879 he died. Yakub Khan, his son and successor as Amir, promptly came to terms with the Viceroy. He agreed to give up control of the Khyber Pass and other border territories and to consult Britain over foreign affairs. Sir Louis Cavagnari, a former Indian Army soldier turned diplomat, was sent to Kabul as British Resident to ensure that the Afghans complied with the terms. He was greeted by an Afghan band playing a barely recognisable rendition of 'God Save the Queen!'

Despite the apparently friendly reception, Cavagnari did not long survive his appointment. On 2 September, a mob of mutinous Afghan soldiers stormed the British Residency, slaughtering the Resident and all his staff. Though a brilliant military campaign led by General Roberts eventually salvaged the situation, British prestige was severely shaken and the repercussions were felt at home and abroad. While it was disputed whether or not Lord Lytton had exceeded his authority as Viceroy of India by acting more or less unilaterally, there was no doubt that the situation had been made worse by dithering in Westminster and Whitehall.

Isandhlwana and Rorke's Drift

Much the same thing was happening far away in South Africa. There, Sir Bartle Frere – a bull-headed but determined imperialist with a distinguished reputation from the Indian Mutiny but no previous African experience – had recently been appointed High Commissioner of the Cape Colony. The first problem he faced was how best to deal with the Zulus, who, according to colonists in Natal, were fast becoming a menace.

In November 1878 Frere was ordered to meet 'the Zulus in a spirit of forbearance and reasonable compromise', but he simply ignored the instruction. Instead, he chose to interpret earlier, more ambiguous despatches from London as giving him authority to proceed as he thought best. He came to the conclusion that, in order to bolster British power and appease the Boers in the Transvaal, who were rapidly becoming restive under British rule, it was necessary once for all to break the power of the Zulu chieftain Cetewayo and the mighty nation of brave warriors that he ruled.

Cetewayo was charismatic, ruthless and a great military leader with a powerful army at his disposal. To deal with him, Frere ordered three invading columns to strike into the heart of Zululand. Commanded by General Lord Chelmsford, a force of 5,000 British troops with 8,200 native levies were initially involved. The plan was for the columns to advance independently and eventually converge on the Royal Kraal at Ulundi, Cetewayo's capital.

BLUNDERER
Sir Bartle Frere, Governor of Cape Colony, had his own ideas about curbing Zulu power and sent them an ultimatum he knew would be rejected.

By 27 January, 1879, the central column, consisting of 1,500 British and 2,500 native troops, had advanced as far as Isandhlwana, where they set up a temporary camp. That morning, while Chelmsford himself was absent, having gone on ahead with a reconnaissance party, the remainder of the force was taken totally by surprise and routed by a Zulu army some 10,000 strong. The casualties were horrendous – 806 British and 471 natives were killed. Only a few got away. It was not Zulu practice to take prisoners.

News of the disaster reached Frere four days later and London by mid-February. The entire country, from the Queen downwards, was utterly dismayed by the news. Nevertheless, she urged the government 'not to be downhearted for a moment, but show a brave front to the world' until the 'honour of Great Britain' had been restored. Disraeli was equally appalled. 'The terrible disaster,' he wrote to Lady Chesterfield, 'has shaken me to the centre.'

Meanwhile, some 3,000 to 4,000 Zulus, led by Cetewayo's brother, had marched on a position the British had taken up at Rorke's Drift, just across the frontier. It was held by around 80 fit men, with 40 more in hospital accommodation that had been set up there. There was some native support, but at the first sight of the advancing Zulu impis, 'the Kaffirs,' as one British soldier contemptuously called them, 'bolted towards Halpmakaar and what was worse their officer and a European sergeant went with them'. The tiny British garrison was left to fend for itself.

The Zulus attacked the position six times, but each time they were repulsed. They withdrew at dawn the following day. British losses totalled 17 dead and 10 wounded. It took until July for Cetewayo to be brought to bay outside his capital. He was defeated and the Zulu army destroyed.

THE ZULU WAR
British troops parade in their camp at Port Elizabeth, Cape Province, South Africa. They were expected to win a quick and easy victory over the Zulus, led by King Cetewayo (right), but the Zulus struck first. On 22 January, 1879, they almost annihilated a force of around 1,300 British and African troops attempting to defend a temporary base camp at Isandhlwana, just across the Zulu border.

News of the defeat shocked Britain. Five regiments of reinforcements were rushed to the Cape and Chelmsford informed that he would be replaced as British commander. But before his successor could reach South Africa, Chelmsford avenged the defeat when he crushed the Zulu impis at Ulundi, forcing Cetewayo into flight.

The war was over. Cetewayo was eventually captured and, after a period of imprisonment in the Cape, was allowed to visit Britain, where he was received in audience by Queen Victoria. Zululand was split up into small kingdoms. Cetewayo was given one of these to rule, but he was overthrown by a usurper and died in mysterious circumstances shortly afterwards.

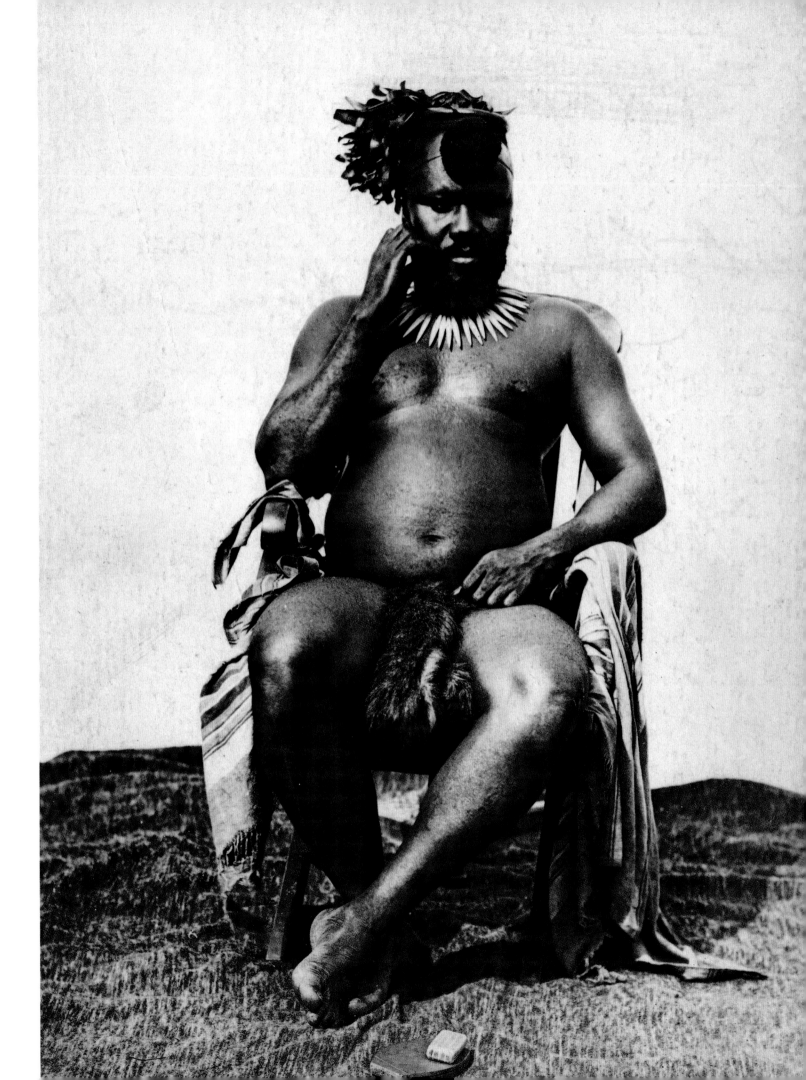

The defensive action at Rorke's Drift was a fine example of British determination and courage on the battlefield in the face of overwhelming odds and it rekindled the morale of the whole nation. To the Victorian, being beaten by European soldiers would have been bad enough – to be trounced by black savages was unthinkable. But success at Rorke's Drift could not alter the fact that the government had blundered into war with the Zulus in the first place. Much to the Queen's displeasure, Lord Chelmsford was made the scapegoat and Sir Garnet Wolseley, hero of the Ashanti Wars, was despatched to South Africa to replace him. In the event, Wolseley arrived after the decisive battle had been fought and won by Chelmsford. Sir Bartle Frere was severely reprimanded, but he was not recalled, much to the dismay of Lord Salisbury who told his young nephew, Arthur Balfour, that 'Bartle Frere should have been recalled as soon as the news of his ultimatum reached England'.

The Queen was determined that lessons should be learned. She lectured the government on the necessity of being continually alert for trouble and ready to deal with it. 'If we are to maintain our position as a first-rate power', she warned Disraeli, 'we must, with our Indian Empire and large colonies, be prepared for attacks and wars, somewhere or other, continually.' The unanswered question was whether the country could be coaxed into higher taxes to pay for the extra military effort. It was one of the great issues of the imperial age, especially at a time of mounting economic recession. It was to remain unresolved.

TRIBAL LEVIES
Native troops in Natal, some armed with modern rifles but the majority with their traditional shields and spears, line up behind their British officers. The British relied on native troops to support their regulars; almost 500 were slaughtered at Isandhlwana alongside the British.

HEROES OF RORKE'S DRIFT
The survivors of B Company 2nd/24th South Wales Borderers, who had successfully defended their position at Rorke's Drift against a much larger attacking force of Zulus, led by King Cetewayo's brother. The action cost the Zulus 3,000 of their best warriors. The astounding bravery of the troops at Rorke's Drift won them 11 Victoria Crosses, one of which went to Major John Chard (left) who commanded the British force in action.

'A very remarkable people the Zulus; they defeat our generals; they convert our bishops; they have settled the fate of a great European dynasty.'

Benjamin Disraeli

HARD
TIMES

By the mid-1870s, Victorian Britain was changing fast. Cheaper food and higher wages affected not only the way in which people lived, but also what they were coming to expect out of life. On returning to power the Conservatives carried through various social reforms, which before long would begin to have an impact. But little of this progress mattered to the worker who had lost his job and could not afford to feed his family.

INNER-CITY GLASGOW Children on the steps of a tenement in 1874; slums like this alley were a Victorian disgrace.

PERMISSION TO IMPROVE

Whether or not Disraeli was a committed, consistent social reformer is a question that has been debated on and off for many years. In his younger days, during the 'Hungry Forties', he was considered to be something of a radical. When he became Prime Minister for the second time, in 1874, conditions in the country had changed and so had he. Now turned 70, he was feeling his age and attempted to keep up appearances by having his hair dyed black. He suffered from asthma, especially on damp days and nights, and frequent debilitating headaches. Painful attacks of gout made it hard for him to walk without the aid of a stick and he took to wearing soft velvet slippers in the House of Commons in an attempt to ease the pain during late night debates.

Letting others lead

Two years previously, during a speech at the Crystal Palace, Disraeli had made the somewhat nebulous pledge to 'elevate the condition of the people'. But now that he was back in power, he seemed to have few ideas to back this up – there was no worked-out, cut-and-dried programme of domestic reforms ready to put forward. Indeed, when it came to drafting the Queen's Speech for the opening of the new Parliament, he and his Cabinet struggled to find enough to put in it.

Richard Cross, a well-to-do banker from Lancashire whom Disraeli propelled from the backbenches into high office as Home Secretary, expressed his personal surprise that the Prime Minister had no real plans to unveil. Cross was, he confessed, 'disappointed at the want of originality shown by the Prime Minister. From all his speeches, I had quite expected that his mind was full of legislative schemes, but such did not prove to be the case. On the contrary, he had to rely on the various suggestions of his colleagues, and they themselves have only just come into office.' But Disraeli was quite ready to let individual ministers proceed as the need arose. 'His mind,' Cross commented, 'was either above or below (whichever way you like to put it) mere questions of detail.'

The birth of Tory democracy

As the reforms of various ministers were pushed through Parliament, what would later be christened Tory democracy was born. Cross was prime mover in the programme. His Artisans' Dwelling Act of 1875 gave local authorities the power to purchase and clear the worst slums. It was followed by a Public Health Act and two Factory Acts. The first Factory Act reduced the maximum number of hours that could be worked in a single shift in the textile mills to 10 and also limited the working week to no more than 56 hours. Children were not allowed to work full time until they were 14, an age limit that would not be raised again until after the Second World War. The second Factory Act brought smaller 'workshops' under the same legislation. The Conspiracy and Protection of Property Act sounded forbidding, but actually legalised peaceful picketing, so settling once and for all, Disraeli hoped, 'the long, vexatious contest between capital and labour'.

MEDIEVAL CONDITIONS
The distinctive spire of St Thomas's Cathedral towers above the crooked, cramped lanes in Newcastle-upon-Tyne. Shipbuilding was the life blood of the city, but as yet no government or political party saw it as its business to ensure adequate housing for workers. The prolific house-building of the Victorian era did more to help the middle classes and better-off working class. Housing for the poor remained a national problem. Social reformer George Sims, the crusading author of *How the Poor Live*, wrote that the London poor 'must put up with dirt, and filth, and putrefaction; with all the nameless abomination of an unsanitary hovel, because if they complain the landlord can turn them out at once, and find dozens of people eager to take their places'.

TORY REFORMER
Richard Assheton Cross, a banker turned Conservative politician, was brought into the Cabinet as Home Secretary when Disraeli formed his second administration in 1874. Cross was given the task of implementing much-needed reforms, one of the most important of which was the 1875 Public Health Act. The legislation was passed, but it was 'permissive' – in other words, voluntary. If local authorities so chose, they could simply ignore the Act altogether and its recommendations.

Disraeli declared that these and the other reforms his government introduced 'would gain and retain for the Conservatives the lasting affections of the working class'. They were certainly well received. A popular chant of the time ran:

'For he's a jolly good fellow, whatever the Rads [radicals] may think,
for he shortened the hours of work, and lengthened the hours of drink!'

One of the government's first measures had been to introduce a Licensing Act, which loosened the restrictions placed on pub opening hours by Gladstone's previous legislation. Simultaneously pandering to brewers and drinkers would, it was hoped, be a sure-fire vote-winner.

The legislation in practice

Though all this looked well enough on the surface, the reform legislation had a weakness. Much of it was permissive, rather than obligatory. It was left up to local authorities to decide whether to implement or ignore it. In Birmingham, Joseph Chamberlain, the city's young and energetic Lord Mayor, did not hesitate to make use of the new legislation. He recorded how the city was 'parked, paved, assized, marketed, Gas-and-Watered and improved – all as the result of three years' active work!' True to his nickname of 'Radical Joe', Chamberlain used the provisions of the Artisans' Dwelling Act to clear and redevelop some 40 to 50 acres of the city's worst slums. But across the rest of England and Wales, only 10 out of 87 local authorities were prepared to take advantage of the powers the Act had given them.

Similarly, the Food and Drugs Act set out to put a stop to the adulteration of food, a common problem at the time. But the Act was not binding. It did not force local authorities to appoint the chemical analysts necessary to make the law effective, and many elected to do little or nothing. Even in go-ahead Birmingham, Chamberlain had to overcome substantial resistance from the more diehard members of the City Council. They held, for instance, that the appointment of municipal sanitary inspectors – in 1871, the town had one of the worst health records in Britain – was unEnglish, unconstitutional and, as one indignant councillor put it, 'a violation of the sanctity of the home'. Even Cross, the proposer of the legislation, believed that the power of the state to intervene should be limited. 'I take it as a starting point,' he told the House, 'that it is not the duty of the government to provide any class of citizens with any of the necessaries of life'.

'RADICAL JOE'
Birmingham screw-manufacturer Joseph Chamberlain became the city's Lord Mayor in 1873. He was an ardent social reformer who seized on the new permissive reform legislation brought in by the Tories. Under his leadership Birmingham embarked on a massive slum clearance and re-housing project, and won renown as 'the best governed City in the World'. In 1876 he entered Parliament as a Liberal MP for Birmingham and became an outspoken leader of the radical wing of the Party.

'It is always cheaper to pay labour its full value .... Labour should be paid better than thieving. At present, it pays worse.'
Florence Nightingale

Laissez-faire rules

Overall, the philosophy of *laissez-faire* remained the order of the day. It was an article of faith held by practically everybody that, at most, governments should only lay down guidelines for improvements. Other bodies would decide whether to act on them or ignore them. Speaking in support of the Agricultural Holdings Bill, designed to provide tenant-farmers with compensation for any improvements they made to their farms, Disraeli summed up the principle behind his government's approach. 'Permissive legislation,' he explained, was 'characteristic of a free

THREE'S COMPANY
A wall worker (standing) and second-hand clothes dealer (centre) share a pipe and a beer with a friend outside The Wallmaker, a public house in London, in 1877. For many, especially the poor, having a drink was one of life's few pleasures. Gladstone's government had attempted to introduce an unpopular Licensing Act, which went a long way to explaining his inglorious defeat at the polls in 1874. The defeated premier put most of the blame for his overthrow on the brewers, telling his brother Robertson that he had been 'borne down in a torrent of gin and beer'. The replacement legislation of Disraeli's subsequent government was toothless and so less controversial.

people. It is easy to adopt compulsory legislation when you have to deal with those who only exist to obey; but in a free country, and especially in a country like England, you must trust to persuasion and example … if you wish to effect any considerable change in the manner and customs of the people.'

Later, he went further. With the slump at its height, Disraeli adhered strictly to the prevailing economic orthodoxy, rejecting any idea of intervention. In December 1878 he told Parliament: 'Her Majesty's Government are not prepared – I do not suppose any government would be prepared – with any measures which would attempt to alleviate the extensive distress which now prevails.'

Gladstone, too, had little to offer his beleaguered countrymen but words. Speaking to depression-stricken farmers in Midlothian in 1879, he declared: 'I

THE WANDERING LIFE
A gypsy caravan at an encampment in Battersea, recorded for posterity in *Street Life in London* in 1877. There were similar encampments in Wandsworth, Walworth and Notting Dale. Nomades, as *Street Life* termed them, were a common sight in London's streets, as they would have been in other cities in Victorian times. This particular caravan's owner was William Hampton, who is seated by the steps in the foreground. He enjoyed a reputation amongst his fellows of being 'a fair-spoken, honest gentleman'. As well as attending fairs and markets, gypsies were street traders and sold ornaments and other wares door to door. Most left London for the country in the summer, returning to the capital in October to sell horses and otherwise make a living by hawking clothes pegs, mending pots and pans, telling fortunes and, if all else failed, by begging.

hope it may perhaps be my privilege … to assist in procuring for you some of those provisions of necessary liberation from restraint, but beyond that, it is your own energies, of thought and action, to which you will have to trust.' To an audience of some 4,700 people in Edinburgh's Corn Exchange, he frankly stated that it was 'the mark of a chicken-hearted Chancellor … when he shrinks from upholding economy in detail … [and] even worse than the mismanagement of finance is destruction or disparagement of the sound and healthy rules which the wisdom of a long series of finance ministers has gradually built up to prevent abuse and to take care that the people should not be unduly burdened.'

In the light of such outpourings, *Punch* wittily but affectionately christened Gladstone the 'Colossus of Words.' For him, it was an article of faith that, especially in difficult times, all citizens, from highest to lowest, must look to themselves for help. This was why he sternly warned the inmates of a London workhouse against the temptations of aspiring to what he termed 'luxurious living', counselling against the fallacy of believing that a labourer 'could do better for himself by making himself a charge upon the community'.

continued on page 109

CURE-ALLS
An itinerant vendor of pills, potions and other quack remedies plies his wares from door to door. By 1877, when this picture was taken for *Street Life in London*, such medicament sellers were in decline. The book's authors noted that: 'The increasingly large number of free hospitals, where the poor may consult qualified physicians, the aid received at a trifling cost from clubs and friendly societies, and the spread of education, have all tended to sweep this class of street-folks from the thoroughfares of London.'

THE BOTTOM LINE

A jumble of tugs, tramp steamers and barges lie clustered alongside a wharf in London Docks. Sprawling for miles along the river, the docks were conceived on an imperial scale. One author wrote: 'The extensive basins, in which may be seen the largest ships in the world; the immense warehouses, which contain the treasures of every quarter of the globe – wool, cotton, tea, coffee, tobacco, skins, ivory; the miles of vaults filled with wines and spirits; the thousands of people employed – clerks, customs officers, artisans, labourers, lightermen and sailors – make the Docks a world of itself, as well as a cosmopolitan rendezvous and emporium.'

Britain's merchant marine certainly ruled the waves. Its share of world merchant shipping tonnage rose from 29.5 per cent in 1840 to 35.8 per cent in 1890. It went on increasing right up until 1912, when it was estimated that around half of all the world's seaborne trade was being carried in British vessels. But in the 1870s not all of the ships were seaworthy. Unscrupulous ship-owners, in pursuit of maximum profits, would dangerously overload vessels, which increased the danger of sinking. The Liberal MP Samuel Plimsoll (above) campaigned tirelessly to outlaw the practice of overloading. Eventually he succeeded and legislation was passed that made it compulsory to paint a line – named in his honour the Plimsoll line – on the hull of a cargo ship to indicate how much the vessel could carry in safety.

THE TICHBORNE CLAIMANT – FRAUD OR VICTIM?

Cigar-smoking Arthur Orton, an Australian butcher otherwise known as Tom Castro, rocked British society when he emerged from obscurity to claim to be the long-lost baronet Sir Roger Tichborne and heir to the family fortune. Sir Roger's own mother accepted his claim, but other family members insisted that he was a fraudulent imposter and went to court to prove it.

When the case was heard, in May 1871, more than 100 witnesses vouched for Castro's identity as Sir Roger. But after a mammoth 22-day cross-examination, he lost the case. He was promptly arrested and a second court case ensued. This time he was in the dock as Arthur Orton, accused of perjury. He was convicted and sentenced to 14 years imprisonment with hard labour.

Many people refused to believe that Castro was guilty. Chief among these was his barrister, Dr Edward Kenealy (right), who claimed that his client was the victim of a conspiracy involving the Jesuits – Sir Roger had attended a Jesuit public school – the law lords and others among the highest in the land. One thing the case did do was sell newspapers. The paper-boy below peddles an evening paper with the latest news. Orton was released after serving ten years, by then a broken man.

Only a few of the reforms that the Conservatives passed into law really captured the public imagination, which was not surprising for most of them were worthy but dull. The Tories wanted to avoid potential areas of political controversy. One Conservative MP commented that it was 'suet-pudding legislation; it was flat, insipid, dull, but it was very wise and very wholesome'. Nevertheless, there were some issues over which the public was prepared to be aroused.

The Plimsoll line

Liberal philanthropist and outspoken MP Samuel Plimsoll succeeded in getting the nation behind him. His battle was to save the lives of Britain's sailors, who had been exploited by unscrupulous ship-owners for years. In 1871 alone, the year that Plimsoll embarked on his crusade, a staggering 856 ships were lost within 10 miles of the British coast in conditions no worse than a gentle breeze. Horrified by these deadly statistics, Plimsoll launched a nationwide campaign against what he called 'coffin ships' – decrepit, over-loaded, unseaworthy vessels that were sent to sea regardless of the conditions. Some owners actually over-insured their ships and cargoes in the expectation that they would, more than likely, go to the bottom.

Plimsoll's dedication and sincerity won him massive public support – and the lasting enmity of ship-owners, who sued him for libel on 18 occasions. Matters came to a head in July 1875 when the government, running short of precious Parliamentary time, withdrew its own Merchant Shipping Act, an innocuous measure that Plimsoll had supported for the want of anything better. Storming to his feet in defiance of the Speaker, who ruled him out of order, he bellowed at the top of his voice that he was 'determined to unmask the villains who send our seamen to death and destruction'. A sympathetic American observer commented: 'It was a sort of divine passion, breaking out with thunder and lightning. This man has dwelt on the scene of poor wretches struggling amid the waves to an extent hardly appreciated by the gentlemen of England who live at home at ease.'

> 'There are a thousand lives at stake. You do not know these men as I do.'
>
> **Samuel Plimsoll**

What Plimsoll wanted was simple. It was to have a line painted on the hulls of ships that would be a gauge to check that they were not too heavily laden. Thousands flocked to rallies in his support and even the Queen expressed concern. She told a discomforted Disraeli that 'the state of Merchant Shipping vessels is very disgraceful and dangerous and many lives are lost hereby'. The government found itself press-ganged into introducing legislation that, as Plimsoll himself put it, 'would remedy the evils which afflict our sea-going population'. He was briefly the most popular man in Britain, even though the actual positioning of the Plimsoll line did not become legally binding for another 20 years. One diehard ship-owner showed his contempt by having the line painted on his ships' funnels.

The Tichborne claimant

Plimsoll was not the only figure to capture the popular imagination. The strange story of an Australian butcher who claimed to be the long-lost baronet Sir Roger Tichborne, heir to a vast Hampshire estate, became a *cause célèbre* that divided the entire nation. It culminated in a trial that, for many years, held the record as Britain's longest-running court case. The story began in 1854, when the 25-year-old Sir Roger was reported lost at sea – the boat on which he was sailing sank off

South America, apparently with all hands. Refusing to accept that her son had perished, his mother never gave up hope that he would someday reappear. Some 11 years after the disappearance, she advertised in the Australian press, offering a reward for any sighting of her son. A man calling himself Tom Castro, a butcher from Wagga Wagga, came forward claiming to be the long-lost Sir Roger.

Castro seemed an unlikely candidate. He was extremely stout at 21 stone, and bore only a passing facial resemblance to the pale, skinny aristocrat. Unlike the real Sir Roger, he could not speak French. Nor could he recall anything about Stonyhurst College, the Catholic public school in the north of England that the young Roger had attended. He was also bankrupt and in debt to the lawyer who had first drawn his attention to the advertisement. Nevertheless, Lady Tichborne offered to pay Castro's fare to Britain. When the two met, she declared: 'He looks like his father and he has his uncle's ears.' But though she was prepared to believe Castro's story, other members of the family were not. Nor were many of Sir Roger's former friends. Popular opinion, in contrast, was on Castro's side.

The stage was set for an epic legal battle, which began in 1871 when Castro brought an action in the Court of Common Pleas to establish his rights to the disputed inheritance. The action lasted for 102 days, during which more than 100 witnesses came forward to vouch for his identity as Sir Roger. Not to be outdone, the outraged Tichborne family – old Lady Tichborne had died shortly before the trial started – hired an army of private detectives to probe into Castro's Australian antecedents. They uncovered dramatic new evidence that pointed to Castro being a man called Arthur Orton, who had lived in Wapping in London's East End before emigrating to start a new life in the colonies.

The jury threw out Castro's case. He was promptly arrested and charged – under his real name of Orton – with two counts of perjury. His trial began in

HOME SWEET HOME
The shack in Wagga Wagga, Australia, where Tom Castro lived before travelling to England to attempt to claim the identity and inheritance of Sir Roger Tichborne.

DID SHE DO IT?
Victorians were fascinated by crime, particularly murder. The poisoning of 30-year-old barrister Charles Bravo (right) in 1876 was one of many sensational cases that gripped the nation. His wife Florence (far right), who had married Bravo only five months previously, was the main suspect, together with Jane Cox, her companion. But despite two inquests – the first returned an open verdict, the second 'wilful murder' – nothing could ever be proved against the two women. Florence died of drink two years after her husband's death.

Three years earlier, Mary Ann Cotton had been the name in the headlines. Using a series of false names, she left a trail of at least 21 dead bodies behind her, including her mother, three of her four husbands, at least one lover, and a number of her own children and stepchildren. Eventually, a suspicious doctor insisted on a post-mortem being carried out on one of her stepsons. Arsenic was detected in the dead boy's stomach. Mary Ann was tried and hanged in Durham Prison.

1873 and lasted for a mammoth 188 days. It ended with a guilty verdict and a sentence of 14 years hard labour. Yet despite seemingly irrefutable evidence against him, many ordinary people believed Castro to be the victim of an aristocratic conspiracy. For months, newspapers were full of little else. Tichborne societies sprang up throughout the land, demonstrating in his support and raising funds to help him with his claim. News of the story even reached far-away Naples, where the San Carlo Opera House announced a new opera – *Roger di Ticciborni*.

Dr Edward Kenealy, the fiery Irish lawyer who had acted for Castro in both court cases, stood in a by-election in Stoke-on-Trent on a platform totally devoted to Castro's cause. He trounced both the Conservative and Liberal candidates and entered the House of Commons in February 1875. Upon his arrival he immediately demanded that a Royal Commission be set up to look into the conduct of Castro's trial – Kenealy's own behaviour in court had led to him being struck off the list of Queen's Counsel and disbarred as a barrister – and to determine his client's guilt or innocence. The motion was defeated by an overwhelming 433 votes to three. Castro served 10 years, eventually emerging from prison a broken and almost forgotten man.

continued on page 114

KEEPING WATCH
Charles Rouse, the last of the night-watchmen known as Charlies, poses for the camera on his beat along London's Brixton Road in 1875. Charlies were first introduced into the capital by Charles II, from whom they got their name. By Victorian times, with the arrival of a proper police force, they were fast becoming obsolete. Sir Matthew Wood, the Lord Mayor of London, accused them of spending the time they should have been patrolling playing cards, drinking in pubs or simply fast asleep.

EXPEDITION TO THE ARCTIC

THE FROZEN NORTH

The Victorians were many things, but above all they were great explorers. While missionary David Livingstone was penetrating into the heart of the Dark Continent, as Africa was commonly known, another intrepid Victorian adventurer, Captain George Nares (left), was ordered back from Hong Kong by the Admiralty and sent out on a new mission to reach the North Pole. Nares had served on an earlier voyage to survey the Arctic. Having risen to the rank of captain, he was now an obvious choice to head up the latest adventure. With two ships under his command – HMS *Alert* and HMS *Discovery* (top left) – his orders were to sail up the west coast of Greenland via Smith Sound and the Kennedy Channel, where, so the Admiralty believed, an open sea would give a clear route to the Pole.

A 200,000-strong crowd turned out to cheer as Nares set sail from Portsmouth in May 1875. All went well at first, but once they arrived in the Arctic, the expedition soon hit bad weather. Both ships became trapped – the *Alert* is shown above, with her crew attempting to fish through holes cut in the ice. The crew did manage to hunt and kill a walrus for food (far left), but without enough fruit and vegetables on board to survive a long ice-bound winter, the men faced the deadly peril of scurvy.

The expedition's equipment also proved inadequate. The sledges were too heavy for the men to pull, their Arctic clothing was too tight and restrictive, and their tents were altogether hopeless – they were too small and did not keep out the wind, the driven snow or the cold.

Eventually, with many among the crews of both ships falling sick, Nares sailed for home. Though he and his men had struggled valiantly, they had not found a way to the Pole. 'No one,' wrote Lieutenant Beaumont, in charge of one of the mapping parties, 'will ever be able to understand what work we have had during those days, but the following may give some idea of it. When we halted for lunch, two of the men crept on all fours for 200 yards, rather than walk through that terrible snow.'

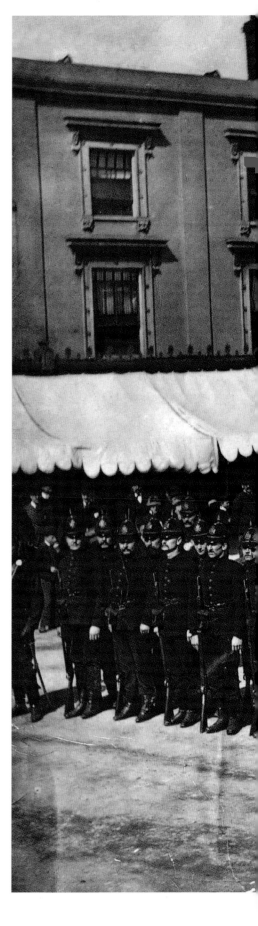

DEFENDING THE REALM
A contingent of the St George's Rifles stands on parade in the early 1870s. The men in the ranks were not regular soldiers, they were part-time volunteers. The force came into existence because many thought that the country faced the threat of French invasion. No less a personage than Tennyson had penned a poem, printed in *The Times*, calling for volunteers to help defend the country should the forces of Napoleon III actually attack. Meanwhile, the regular army was busy fighting abroad. From the 1860s onwards, scarcely a year went by when British troops were not in action somewhere in the world.

FACING RECESSION

The economic confidence – some said complacency – that characterised the first years of the decade was starting to give way to doubt and uncertainty. After a period of explosive boom, the economy was now slowing as its rate of growth fell. Increased competition from manufacturers abroad – notably in the USA and Germany – was beginning to affect the export trade on which British prosperity depended, forcing down the prices that could be charged for the nation's industrial products. Over the 30 years prior to 1870, the value of British exports had expanded at an average of 5 per cent per annum. From 1870 to 1890, that rate of growth slumped to 2 per cent a year. The annual value of the nation's exports would not regain the levels of the early 1870s until 1895.

Hard times had arrived and it seemed there was little, if anything, that the government was prepared to do about it. Putting up taxes in order to pay for relief measures was anathema to politicians of all parties. Nor was the imposition of protective tariffs considered feasible, even though this was precisely the method by which the USA and Germany chose to protect their own burgeoning industries from competition. As far as Britain's politicians were concerned, even attempting to follow suit would be political suicide, as it would mean disowning the fundamental principles of Free Trade, the pet Victorian sacred cow.

Employers had their own answer: they cut wages. Between 1873 and 1879, the worst year of the slump, wages fell by 5 per cent in real terms. At the same time, unemployment rose to unprecedented levels. In 1878-9, it was reckoned that more than 11 per cent of the working population was unemployed.

The plight of the poor

Poverty, of course, was endemic in Victorian times, as were long hours of work in often appalling conditions. It was only in 1875, for instance, that the practice of sending small children up chimneys to sweep them free of soot was finally outlawed. Two years previously, Charles Lowder, the vicar of St Peter's, a mission church in Wapping in the heart of London's docklands, had recorded how the poorest of his parishioners were 'for weeks, sometimes months without work, and unable to support their families. Their clothes, their furniture, their bedding, all pawned, they lay on bare beds, or on the floor, only kept warm by being huddled together in one closed, unventilated room.'

In industrial areas, conditions were no better – often worse. In the first six months of 1875, the South Wales coalfields lay idle, brought to a standstill by a

UP THE CHIMNEY

John Day (left), captured here with one of his children, was known in his neighbourhood as 'the temperance sweep' because, unlike many of his fellow chimney sweeps, he had succeeded in giving up drinking and smoking. Chimney sweeps, carrying their rods and brushes on their shoulders, were a common sight in town and city streets; in London alone, it was estimated that there were at least 2,000 of them. It was now an adult trade; the barbarous practice of using small children to climb up inside chimneys was finally outlawed by Parliament in 1875. Depending on the height of the chimney and the prosperity of the locality, charges ranged from 6d to 3 shillings. The cost of putting out a chimney fire, a regular occurrence, was generally 5 shillings.

CHILDREN'S SAVIOUR

Dr Thomas Barnardo (below), founder of the children's homes that still bear his name, led a crusade to rescue destitute boys and girls from living rough on the streets. In the course of his work, he would raise the enormous sum of £3.25 million to finance his endeavours. This enabled him to save no fewer than 60,000 children from penury. Barnardo opened his first home for boys in London's East End in 1870. By the end of the decade, 50 such orphanages had been established for boys and girls. Above each one, a sign declared 'No Destitute Child Ever Refused Admission'.

pay dispute following two wage reductions imposed on the miners by the colliery owners. Radical MP Alexander Macdonald bitterly denounced 'the great families of Wales', whom he accused of enrichening themselves at the expense of the workers, warning that they 'would go down to posterity with infamy as poltroons who attacked women and children'.

Cutting wages did nothing to remedy the situation. From the end of 1875 until the beginning of 1880, the selling price of coal went steadily down. Other staple industries in the region also suffered. In South Wales, the amount of pig iron smelted fell from nearly 715,000 tons in 1874 to about 670,000 tons in 1879, largely because of the collapse of the export trade in rails to the US railroad, which itself had entered recession. In 1877 the huge Aberdare Valley iron works closed down, and many others in the region were also soon forced to quench their furnaces. Lying idle, deserted and desolate, they looked, said one observer, like 'gaunt and silent spectres'.

In Lancashire, where Britain's great cotton mills were the main employer, the poor relief statistics told a tale of increasing misery. In the Salford workhouse in 1874, the year in which Disraeli took office, there were 851 inmates and 1,922 people receiving outdoor relief. By 1 January, 1880, the number of inmates had increased slightly to 867, but the numbers on outdoor relief had shot up by almost

FLOOD VICTIMS
Poor Londoners driven from their homes by a Thames flood in 1877, photographed in front of a rag shop in Lambeth. Flooding at times of exceptionally high tide was an annual occurrence, but the Metropolitan Board of Works claimed that it lacked the necessary funds to finance remedial action. Eventually, MPs intervened. After two years of talk, the Thames River (Prevention of Floods) Bill was passed in the teeth of fierce opposition from property owners along the river, who regarded the extra levies they would have to pay as 'unfair and unjust'.

50 per cent to 2,838. The local Liberals were quick to point out the obvious message. 'So much for Tory rule, with its bad trade, heavy rates and taxes', read a leaflet of the day. 'If you have not had enough of these, vote for the Tories!'

Agriculture in decline

Farmers were among the worst hit. Three consecutive years of bad harvests culminated in a total failure in 1879, when practically the entire cereal crop was wiped out in what was then the wettest summer on record. Normally, farmers should at least have benefited from a consequent rise in prices, but now foreign imports – particularly from the USA, which could export corn at prices that undercut British farmers at the best of times – were keeping prices well below 1873 levels. In that year, the cost of sending a ton of grain from Chicago to Liverpool was £3 7s; by the end of the decade, this had fallen to just £1 4s. The price of British wheat was forced down from 56s 9d per quarter in 1877 to 46s 5d only a year later – and then to an all-time low of 31s a quarter. The consequences

VICTIMS OF THE SLUMP
Workers at the Millwall Iron Works, Ship Building & Graving Docks Company, hard by the Thames in the East End of London, take a break for the camera in the 1870s. It was here that the *Great Eastern*, Brunel's greatest steamship, had been built two decades previously. At its peak, the company employed between 4,000 and 5,000 men, who enjoyed remarkably enlightened conditions for the day, including a half-day on Saturday, a canteen, sports clubs and works band. The company eventually collapsed, a victim of the financial crisis and economic recession.

were catastrophic. Between 1870 and 1900, some 400,000 jobs were permanently lost in farming as thousands of labourers were forced off the land. Many farmers went bankrupt and land that could not be farmed profitably was allowed to fall fallow. In less than a decade, the amount of land devoted to wheat cultivation shrank by a staggering million acres. Small wonder that Dorset born-and-bred novelist Thomas Hardy, whose first big success came with *Far From the Madding Crowd* in 1874, should later make the perils of corn farming and corn dealing the central theme of *The Mayor of Casterbridge*, a tragic portrayal of the rise and fall of corn merchant Michael Henchard, the Mayor of the novel's title.

In hard-hit Hertfordshire, one farm forced onto the market 'in consequence of the depressed state of agriculture' was offered at the 'very low rent of £78pa, previous to which it was let for £105pa'. Yet even with this drastic reduction in rent there were few, if any, takers, so the advertisers looked beyond the farm's agricultural potential to try to attract interest. 'It is well calculated for a Hunting Box', they boasted, 'being within easy reach of the Hertfordshire and Puckeridge foxhounds.' A similar ploy had been used to try to sell the Temple Disley estate in the same county. Rather than highlighting its farms, the estate deliberately promoted the great opportunities it provided for hunting, shooting and fishing enthusiasts. 'It is in a favourite hunting district,' the particulars claimed, 'the sporting capabilities are of a high character and afford excellent partridge and pheasant shooting.'

continued on page 128

'GOD'S WONDERFUL RAILWAY'
Men at work in the giant Great Western Railway works at Swindon. The Great Western linked London with Bristol, Exeter and points west and was given its nickname by its loyal employees. Railways were the great Victorian success story. By 1870, few towns of any size lacked a station, while cheap rail travel was bringing a new dimension to everyday life. Both suburban commuting and trips to the seaside were given a tremendous boost. In the long run, fast cheap transport of the kind the railways provided helped to reduce the overall cost of living, especially when combined with rising national productivity. And the railways themselves were great employers: 275,000 people worked in the rail industry in 1875.

FRESH FISH FOR THE TABLE

Piles of freshly-caught fish from the North Sea at Lowestoft fish market on the Suffolk coast in the 1870s. From there, sorted and swathed in blocks of ice, it would be whisked away on the Great Eastern Railway. The railways were a huge boon to suppliers of fresh foods of all descriptions, as they greatly speeded up the time it took to get produce into the nation's homes.

Fish featured on the menu in well-to-dp households practically every day of the week. For breakfast, for instance, grilled fish, kippers or kedgeree were served, followed by eggs, bacon, kidneys, sausages and mushrooms, with cold ham or tongue on the side. Dinner-time favourites included fried cod with oyster sauce and lobster cutlets, which were chopped lobster patties.

For more formal occasions, the Victorians could really push the boat out. In 1879, Marion Sambourne, an upper middle-class woman living in leafy Kensington, recorded what she served at a dinner party for eight – her records show that the recession left some people completely unscathed. The meal started with artichoke soup, followed by fillets of salmon. Then came leg of lamb, salad, new potatoes and stewed celery; wild duck and watercress; Aldershot pudding and plum pudding; to round off, a savoury of soft roes of herring and biscuits.

For one of her husband's 'gentlemen only' dinners, Mrs Sambourne truly excelled herself. The menu had caviar as an appetiser; clear soup; cold salmon; pigeons; tomato salad; roast lamb with peas and haricots verts; roast chicken, salad and Russian salad; jelly and a macedoine of fruit; an anchovy savoury; cream cheese; ices and a sorbet; and grapes, cherries and greengages. The 12 diners washed down their food with 15 bottles of Champagne, 12 bottles of Ayala '80, five bottles of Geister '74, two Sauternes and three Burgundy. Little wonder that her husband recorded the following evening that he was suffering from a 'slight bilious headache, which lasted all day.'

BRADBEER
CREAT EASTERN RAILWAY OFFICE
POST OFFICE
TELEGRAPH OFFICE
R.&F. CAPPS
R.&F. CAPPS
LOWESTOF

FARMERS AND FARMING

By the late 1870s, British farming was deep in the throes of depression, due largely to the impact of Free Trade, which made it cheaper to import wheat than to grow it at home. Nearly a million farm labourers left the land. Many emigrated, while others moved into the cities and towns. Life was tough for those who remained. New machinery began to improve the economic efficiency of farming, but was not always popular.

BETTER DAYS
A farm worker and boy pose by an empty cart in front of a once-grand building now pressed into service as a barn. Captured in 1870, by the end of the decade they would count themselves lucky if they were still employed. On the farms, landlords ruled; in 1873, more than two-fifths of the land in England and Wales was owned by fewer than 1,700 people.

TOUGH TIMES AHEAD
A shepherd near Ambleside in the Lake District waits for the ferry to take his small flock across the water. Sheep-farming was one of the major casualties of the depression years. Persistent wet weather from 1878 to 1882 led to an outbreak of liver-rot in places as far apart as Somerset and the Lincolnshire Fens. It is estimated that the disease killed around 4 million sheep.

REAPING WHAT IS SOWN

Farm hands pitch hay into a wagon on a farm near Whitby in Yorkshire. The scene looks idyllic – and haymaking, when the weather was kind, was one of the pleasantest jobs in farming – but, in reality, the conditions for farmers and farm workers were about to get very tough indeed. Poor harvests for several years in the decade – 1873, 1875, 1876 and in particular 1879 – were only part of the problem. Agricultural recession was compounded by a massive increase in imports of foreign wheat and corn, largely from North America.

Disraeli's government recognised that there was a crisis, but failed to take any action. All it offered were words, and even then did not always sound sympathetic. Speaking to the West Hertfordshire Agricultural Society in the Watford Corn Exchange in 1879, Lord Salisbury, Disraeli's Foreign Secretary, confidently assured his audience that 'when the stress of the present pressure should have passed, landlords and tenants alike would look back upon this evil time as one that stimulates their energies'. With sentiments like these being expressed by one of the two leading candidates to succeed the ailing Prime Minister, few could be surprised that the subsequent General Election saw the Liberals returned to power.

MEETING POINT
A group of workers pose in front of an open-sided farm building on a large English farm. The hours of work were long and hard. One Lincolnshire labourer complained of the 'constant grind, month in, month out, with never an hour to call their own'. Farmers and landlords gave short thrift if such complaints were made to their face. It was said of the workers on Lord Wantage's Berkshire estate that 'they dare not blow their noses without the bailiff's leave'.

STEAM POWER
A straw-burning steam plough stands ready for despatch. The plough was made by John Fowler & Co, a Leeds-based engineering company. Steam-driven machines were intended to make farming more efficient, and by the 1870s two-thirds of all corn in the country was being cut and threshed by steam threshers. Steam ploughs proved uneconomical except in large rectangular fields, which prompted the remodelling of many farms to suit the machines.

G. Wormald (Photo)
Leeds.

118

'The corn counties were stricken, it seemed, beyond recovery. Great wars have been less destructive of wealth than the calamity which stretches from 1879, the wettest, to 1894, the driest, year in memory.'

G. M. Young, historian

UNION MAN
Joseph Arch, a farm labourer turned Methodist preacher, came to prominence in early 1872, when he urged a meeting of more than 1,000 fellow farm-workers in Warwickshire to join him in forming a trade union. Over the next few months, the movement spread like wildfire through the Midlands and the eastern counties. In May 1872 the Agricultural Labourers' Union was established, with Arch as its first chairman. By the end of the year membership had reached 40,000, and continued to grow to a peak of 86,200 in 1874.

At first the union was effective in improving wages for its members, but in summer 1874 farmers across the Midlands and East Anglia began a lockout of Union members. The bubble had burst. By late July, the Union was forced to admit defeat and its membership started to decline dramatically. By 1879, it had only 20,000 members; a decade later, the figure was 4,254. Joseph Arch went on to blaze another trail, being elected as an MP in 1885, the first agricultural labourer to do so. This picture shows him in the 1890s, after he had taken a seat on the Liberal benches.

At the same time that the price of corn was heading downwards in what looked like free fall, the nation's cattle and sheep farmers were suffering from an equally disastrous series of natural calamities. In 1877 rinderpest (cattle plague) and pleuropneumonia – both killer conditions – struck so severely that Disraeli's reluctant government had to agree to restrict the movement of cattle and pay compensation to the owners of slaughtered beasts in order to check the spread of infection. Then came a seemingly uncontrollable outbreak of foot-and-mouth disease, and from 1878 an epidemic of liver-rot among sheep. Somerset, north Dorset and the Lincolnshire marshes were the areas worst affected.

Despite all the problems, many farmers survived. Some even increased their profits by switching from growing corn, oats, barley and other cereal crops to meat production and by producing more vegetables and dairy products. New machinery helped to improve farming efficiency and cut labour costs. But for agricultural labourers who survived the import of machinery, wages still fell. 'I doubt', wrote Henry Snell, a farm labourer's son who became an author, a prominent Fabian and eventually an early Labour politician, 'whether men and women ever worked harder and I do not believe that necessary and honourable toil was ever more inadequately rewarded.'

The stark choice – leave or starve

In 1872 Joseph Arch, also the son of a farm labourer, launched the National Agricultural Labourers' Union. Within two years, the union had recruited 86,200 members, a tenth of Britain's rural workforce. Despite substantial opposition from farmers and landowners, Arch and his followers succeeded in raising wages over a wide area of the country by an average of 1s 6d or 2s a week, and in some places by as much as 3s or even 4s. Now came the backlash as wages fell by as much as they had risen – and then by still more.

The outlook was bleak in the extreme. Many labourers were forced to leave the land for the towns or to emigrate. Nearly a million people left England and Wales during the course of the 1870s, many of them destined for Canada and

POORER STILL AND POORER
An Irish peasant family haul creels and sacks of peat home to be burned as their sole source of domestic fuel. All over rural Ireland, small tenant-famers were driven off the land by high rents. Falling into arrears with the rent was almost certain to lead to eviction. Violence was the inevitable result. As agitation spread across Ireland, the universal cry was for lower rents.

Australia. The alternative was slow starvation. Canon Girdlestone, the vicar of Halberton – a large parish in north Devon stretching from Tiverton almost to the Somerset border – organised the move of between 400 and 500 farm-workers and their families to towns and factories in the north of England or to more prosperous parts of the country, such as Kent, where a living wage could still be obtained. In Devon, despite working a ten-and-a-half hour day, a farm labourer was paid as little as 7s or 8s a week – not enough to support a family.

Girdlestone wrote to *The Times* to publicise his parishioners' plight. He described how 'almost everything had to be done for them, their luggage addressed, their railway tickets taken, and full plain directions given to the simple travellers written on a piece of paper in a large and legible hand.' Conditions in other parts of the country were even worse; some crofters in the Scottish Highlands were living on as little as £8 a year.

BULLY TURNED VICTIM
Retired army captain Charles Boycott became the land agent in charge of Lord Erne's estate in County Mayo in 1873. As the depression bit deep at the end of the decade, the newly formed Land League demanded that landlords reduce their rents. When Boycott refused and attempted to force tenants in arrears off their farms, he became the first to feel the effects of a new tactic recommended to the local Irish community by Charles Parnell – they ostracised him. Bernard H Becker, a special correspondent for the *Daily News*, recorded that 'not a soul will sell him sixpence worth of anything'. Boycott was forced to bring in workers from Ulster to harvest his crops, an action that in turn forced the government to send troops to protect them. Before long the silent hostility and noncooperation of the Irish drove Boycott out of the country altogether. Becker told his readers that 'neither he nor his auxiliaries [from Ulster] would be safe for a single hour after the departure of the military'. The captain's name entered the language and the tactic of boycotting has been used many times since to achieve political ends.

Irish unrest

In Ireland, the harsh realities of the depression struck home particularly hard. Faced with falling rents, many landlords – the majority not even resident in the country – took heartless action. They started to evict their existing tenants, reorganising their holdings into larger ones that could be rented out more profitably. This was bad news for tenant farmers and peasants alike – especially for the latter, since they could no longer obtain the migrant work on which they relied. The situation was made even worse by the unexpected return of the potato blight that had triggered the great Irish famine in the 1840s.

As the number of evictions mounted, so, too, did unrest. Michael Davitt, a former member of the Irish Republican Brotherhood, formed the Land League in October 1879 with Charles Stuart Parnell to defend tenants and their rights. They called for the land to be nationalised. The League's Declaration of Principles stated: 'The land of Ireland belongs to all the people of Ireland to be held and cultivated for the sustenance of those whom God declared to be the inhabitants thereof!' The demand for Home Rule was just around the corner.

Agitators supporting the aims of the Land League were soon active as they began organising attacks on property. The resulting Land War, as it came to be known, lasted from 1879 to 1882. Thousands of tenants joined the cause, many of them adopting the tactic of boycotting their landlords by refusing to cooperate with them, their land agents or any incoming new tenants.

Disraeli's decline

No British government of the day could possibly have acceded to the Irish demands and Disraeli's was no exception. Despite his impressive foreign policy and continued popularity with the Queen – who had offered to elevate him from Earl of Beaconsfield to Duke (Disraeli declined) – the worsening depression at home led to a dramatic decline in his public popularity and in that of the Conservatives as a whole. Even the farmers, traditionally a bulwark of Conservative support, began to turn against them. A Farmer's Alliance, formed in July 1879, began to put up its own candidates at by-elections demanding government assistance and a return to economic protectionism.

What the country was looking for was an alternative leader. With the volcanic emergence of Gladstone from retirement, it found one. Even though Gladstone had no more economic remedies to put forward than the Tories, he had a cause with which to rally not only the Liberal party but the nation as a whole.

LAND LEAGUER
Michael Davitt, co-founder of the Land League in 1879 together with Charles Parnell, led their supporters in a struggle against rapacious landlords. The League demanded fairer treatment, and especially lower rents, for all tenant-farmers as a step towards the nationalisation of Irish land.

Davitt was born during the Great Famine of the 1840s. He had experienced eviction as a boy, when his parents were driven off their smallholding in County Mayo. They migrated to Lancashire, where the young Davitt went to work in a factory. There, aged just 11, he lost an arm in an accident. With such a background, it was hardly surprising that Davitt drifted into Fenian politics when he grew up. After serving a sentence in Dartmoor for gun-running, he returned to his homeland and took up the Irish tenants' cause.

'The downfall of Beaconsfieldism is like the vanishing of some vast magnificent castle in an Italian romance. It is too big, however, to be all taken in at once.'

William Ewart Gladstone

CHANGING WORLDS

Women's education took a giant stride forward. In Cambridge, Girton and Newnham Colleges were founded, though their students were not yet allowed to take degrees. Oxford followed shortly afterwards. In politics, Gladstone exploded from retirement. His demagogic campaign won him the Scottish constituency of Midlothian from the Tories and transformed the way in which political leaders fought elections for good and all.

MODEL ROYAL The Princess of Wales in her Doctor of Music robes. The young George Bernard Shaw commented it was a scandal that a supposedly prestigious degree had been awarded for 'playing the piano a little'.

GLADSTONE BOUNCES BACK

Gladstone's sudden retirement from the Liberal leadership had been triggered by his landslide defeat in the General Election in 1874. According to Queen Victoria, in his farewell audience with her he said that his downfall was 'the greatest expression of public disapprobation of a government that he ever remembered' and that accordingly he intended to quit political life for good. In January 1875 he wrote to Lord Granville, the Liberal leader in the House of Lords, to tell him that he saw 'no public advantage in continuing to act as the leader of the Liberal Party' and therefore he felt 'entitled to retire on the present opportunity.' Some 42 years of 'laborious public life' seemed to be at an end.

In Gladstone's absence, the Liberal leadership was divided between Lord Hartington in the House of Commons and Lord Granville in the Lords. The question on everyone's lips, though, was whether or not Gladstone would stick to his decision. For some months, it looked as though he would. Cloistered at Hawarden, his comfortable country retreat in Flintshire, he was occupied with a pamphlet war against the Roman Catholic Church and its pretensions, which he launched in a delayed reaction to the Pope's declaration of papal infallibility. Then, almost as suddenly as he had retired, he plunged back in to active politics.

Passion politics

It was the 'Bulgarian horrors,' as he called them – the massacre of Christian Bulgars by Turkish irregulars – that propelled Gladstone once more to the forefront of political life. Though public indignation at events in the Balkans did not last – especially after Disraeli proclaimed that he had brought back 'peace with honour' from the Congress of Berlin – Gladstone was not to be pacified. Determined to overthrow what he derisively termed Beaconsfieldism, he started to look for a parliamentary constituency from which to launch an all-out assault on Disraeli and all his works. He had already decided that he never wanted to contest his ungrateful two-member seat at Greenwich again – at the 1874 General

GRAND OLD MAN OF POLITICS
The veteran Liberal leader William E Gladstone, pictured standing contendedly in the bosom of his family on the terrace of Hawarden Castle, their Flintshire home. His wife Catherine is seated in the centre of the group. Gladstone wears the characteristic high collar to which he gave his name. After his crushing defeat by Disraeli and the Conservatives in the 1874 General Election, Gladstone resolved that he would only return to active politics in 'exceptional circumstances'. In 1878 he decided those circumstances had arrived.

Election, he had been beaten into second place by a Conservative brewer. He now had two offers before him, one in Leeds and the other from Midlothian in Scotland. After much deliberation, he chose the latter.

The Midlothian campaign

At first sight, Gladstone's decision was surprising. Leeds was a Liberal stronghold with almost 50,000 voters, many them recently enfranchised industrial workers. Midlothian – or Edinburghshire, as it was officially known – was a Conservative seat with an electorate of just 3,620. Gladstone was persuaded to fight in Midlothian by the youthful Lord Rosebery, who at 32 years old was the coming man among a new generation of Liberals.

Rosebery promised to stage-manage the entire campaign and was as good as his word. He invited Gladstone to stay at Dalmeny, his imposing home just outside Edinburgh, and use it as his headquarters for a fortnight's intensive tour of the new constituency. Drawing on experiences of electioneering in the USA – in 1873 he had witnessed the Democratic National Convention in New York – Rosebery meticulously planned every detail of the campaign. His aim was to ensure a spectacular triumph for his revered chief, something that would capture the imagination of folk across the nation, far beyond the boundaries of Midlothian.

Rosebery succeeded brilliantly. Even as Gladstone and his wife travelled to the constituency on their first visit in late November 1879, they were greeted at every stop the train made along the way by cheering crowds clamouring for a speech. The Grand Old Man, as Gladstone was fast becoming known, was happy to oblige from a platform at the back of his new-fangled American-designed Pullman carriage. The scenes at Edinburgh's Waverley Station were extraordinary. The seven-mile route from the station to Rosebery's home was lined with crowds, lighting up the way with burning torches. Fireworks exploded in the night sky. Celebratory bonfires blazed in the fields. 'I have never gone through a more extraordinary day', Gladstone recorded in his diary that night.

From triumph to triumph

The enthusiasm mounted to fever pitch the following day as Gladstone and Rosebery drove through packed streets to the Music Hall in George Street, the venue for the first public meeting of the campaign. Over 70 reporters were gathered in the Upper Gallery, waiting to convey what the Grand Old Man had to say to the nation. He did not disappoint: his oration lasted for two hours as he denounced Disraeli and his government for extravagance, arrogance, dishonouring the constitution and damaging Britain's international reputation by its conduct of foreign and imperial affairs. The British invasion of Afghanistan came in for particular condemnation. In a later speech, he accused Disraeli of endangering world peace 'and all the most fundamental interests of Christian society'.

Triumph succeeded triumph as the tour continued. Gladstone called it a 'festival of freedom' – Disraeli preferred a 'pilgrimage of passion'. It culminated with a monster meeting in Glasgow's St Andrew's Hall on 5 December. The hall was packed to its capacity of 6,500 people; 70,000 had applied for tickets. A second visit to Midlothian the following March, immediately before the General Election, was just as successful. Gladstone's volcanic energy transformed the political landscape of Britain.

continued on page 140

HUSTLE AND BUSTLE
Traffic bustles along King William Street in the heart of the City of London. The area has a place in history – it was just off King William Street in Pudding Lane that the Great Fire broke out in a bakery in 1666. By the 1870s, London was being transformed, due in large part to the coming of the railway. According to one commentator, London was being reduced 'to the condition of a city in a state of siege … invaded on every side by railway directors'. It became 'a very city of hoardings.' In Farringdon alone, some 5,000 people were turned out of their homes as demolition crews and then builders moved in; forced to look for somewhere else to live, they 'thrust into any hole or corner they could put their heads.'

A VICTORIAN EPIC – RAISING CLEOPATRA'S NEEDLE

Erected on the Thames Embankment in London in September 1878, the Egyptian obelisk known as Cleopatra's Needle is not, in fact, connected with Cleopatra at all. It was created for Pharaoh Thutmose III in 1460 BCE, more than a millennium before Cleopatra's day. The monument's only link with the famous Egyptian queen is that prior to its removal to London it stood in Alexandria, her royal capital.

Why and how the giant stone monument was brought to London is a vivid testament to Victorian pride and enterprise. It seems that the British were on the look-out for something suitably Egyptian to commemorate Nelson's great victory, many years before, at the Battle of the Nile during the Napoleonic Wars. Eventually, their eyes came to rest on Cleopatra's Needle.

A public subscription raised £15,000 to pay for the cost of transporting the obelisk from Egypt. Archaeologists supervised its removal from the original site (top left) and the careful encasing of the stone (centre left) in preparation for its transportation to London. Much of the money went on constructing a special cigar-shaped container ship, which would be towed back to Britain. Aptly enough, the container was christened *Cleopatra*. It is seen here loaded with its precious cargo (bottom left), ready to begin its epic sea journey.

The voyage did not lack incident. In the stormy Bay of Biscay, *Cleopatra* seemed in danger of sinking. The captain of *Olga*, the ship towing her, saw no alternative but to rescue *Cleopatra*'s crew and cut the container adrift. The first boat sent out on the rescue mission, manned by a crew of six volunteers, was swamped and sank with all hands. A second attempt managed to get *Cleopatra*'s crew safely back on board the *Olga*, and the line was cut. For five days, no one knew whether *Cleopatra* had sunk or not. Then she was spotted, floating peacefully and quite undamaged, off the northern coast of Spain. Another vessel hooked her back up and towed the Needle on the final leg of its journey. Vast crowds cheered its arrival. The obelisk was erected in its new site on the Thames Embankment (right), where it still stands today. The six men who drowned are commemorated on a plaque on the needle.

WOMEN'S SLOW PROGRESS

In his Midlothian addresses, Gladstone frequently referred to the 'gentlemen' in his audiences, but even though his wife and other female members of his family were often beside him on the platform, he never once mentioned 'ladies' at all. At the time, this was not surprising. Advanced thinker though he was in many ways, Gladstone shared the view of the majority of Victorian men – and a large proportion of the women – that a woman's place was in the home. It was a view shared by the Queen, especially when it came to women trying to carve out careers for themselves and demanding the right to vote.

The *Saturday Review* summed up the male view of the woman's role in the words 'married life is a woman's profession'. The only respectable occupation open to middle-class women, assuming they were spinsters, was that of governess. Working-class women were most likely to be domestic servants, factory workers in the textile and clothing industries, or, in the country, farm labourers. They all earned considerably less than their male counterparts. In the textile mills, for instance, women earned little more than half as much as their male colleagues. Outside textiles, young women were paid on average as little as 12s 11d a week.

The Queen was totally opposed to the notion of women attempting to enter the professions. The prospect of female medical students entering the dissecting rooms together with male ones was, she wrote, 'an awful idea'. But she heaped even more condemnation on the pioneer women's suffragists who raised the cry of 'Votes for Women!' It was, said the Queen, a 'mad, wicked folly'. Lady Amberley, whom the Queen was horrified to discover supported the demand, deserved nothing less than 'a good whipping'.

Schools for girls

Yet despite such opinions among people of power and influence, things were starting to move forward. In 1872 the Girls Public Day School Company was founded; by 1895, it had set up 36 schools throughout the land. Its first schools took as their model the North London Collegiate College. This had been founded by the redoubtable Frances Buss as far back as 1850; she remained at the head of the college until her retirement in 1893, just a year before she died.

Buss's close friend was the equally formidable Dorothea Beale, who had become headmistress of Cheltenham Ladies College in 1858, four years after the

> '**I know there is an obscure feeling, a feeling which is ashamed to express itself openly – as if women had no right to care about anything, except how they may be the most useful servants of some men.**'
>
> John Stuart Mill

continued on page 144

DRESSING TO IMPRESS

Three fashionable young ladies pose for the camera, each one holding the obligatory parasol to protect her skin from the sun. The bulky crinolines of earlier Victorian decades had vanished, to be replaced by less cumbersome crinolettes and then by so-called 'dress improvers,' better known today as bustles. These were made of cane or woollen netted fabric, onto which a woman buttoned her dress. A horsehair pad at the small of the back helped to create a 'mermaid's tail', which was the height of fashion in the 1870s.

Most middle-class women were ruled in what they wore – and in almost everything else in their lives – by their position in society and what was considered good taste. The Reverend J P Faunthorpe, a prolific provider of social and domestic advice, thought that 'although it was the duty of girls to be, and look, beautiful,' they would 'never do so if they think too much about it'. For young middle-class women like these, there was not much else to occupy their time. Although educational and work opportunities were beginning to open up, they would not become the norm for women for decades to come. Marriage remained the life option for most Victorian women, and dress and demeanour were props to help find a suitable husband.

A HARD LIFE

Two of Newlyn's legendary fishwives, a favourite subject for West Country artists and photographers. The bonnets they are wearing were called 'gooks'; they were made out of strong cambric-type linen that could be boiled and starched. With the decline of tin mining, fishing became Cornwall's key industry, until tourism took over in turn. The fishing village of Newlyn was particularly fortunate. Artists descended on the place, drawn by what Stanhope Forbes, a founder of what became known as the Newlyn School, described as 'the beauty of this fair district, which charmed us from the first …'

Artists regarded women like these as quaint, the perfect subject matter, but the hardship of the women's lives is etched in their faces. There was no state welfare system to fall back on in hard times and no retirement pension in old age, not even an inadequate one. If a person could no longer work there was only charitable help, the pawnbroker or the workhouse to turn to, though in many areas some support was provided as 'outdoor relief' rather than forcing the destitute poor into the confines of the workhouse itself.

college's foundation. Both women were forthright advocates of a woman's right to a good education, though some found their fervour off-putting. A satirical rhyme of the day, penned by a Clifton schoolmaster when Miss Buss demanded the right to attend a Headmaster's Conference on public examinations, made it clear that he considered them something of an aberration:

> 'Miss Buss and Miss Beale,
> Cupid's darts do not feel,
> How different from us,
> Miss Beale and Miss Buss.'

Doors were starting to open, albeit gingerly, for women in higher education, too. In 1871 there were only four women doctors in the entire country, all of whom had been forced to qualify abroad. In 1874, when the London School of Medicine for Women opened its doors, it faced down the determined opposition of many diehards in the medical profession. Yet it was not until 1893 that women doctors generally were allowed to become members of the British Medical Association.

Scaling the ivory towers

The universities proved a slightly easier nut for women to crack. In 1878 the University of London became the first academic institution in the land to award degrees to women on the same terms as men. When the first women graduates came forward to be honoured at the university's Convocation ceremony, *Punch* marked the appearance of the 'Girl Graduates' with the following lines:

> 'Thus Woman wins, Haul down your flag,
> Oh stern misogynists before her,
> However much a man may brag,
> Of independence, he'll adore her!'

Progress was still far from plain sailing, but attitudes were slowly changing. By the 1890s Gilbert and Sullivan hailed their heroine Princess Zara in *Utopia Limited* as a 'maiden rich in Girton lore' – Girton and Newnham were the first women's colleges established at Cambridge. In contrast, in the play *The Princes*, and the operetta *Princess Ida* which took the earlier play as its basis, librettist Gilbert expressed typical opinions of the 1870s when he sneered at the notion of a woman's college as the 'maddest folly going'.

Oxford followed Cambridge. Lady Margaret Hall and Somerville College were both founded in 1879. But unlike the more forward-looking London University, both Oxford

THREE FEMINIST REFORMERS

Dorothea Beale (left) was a founder student at Queens College for Women when it opened in Harley Street, London, in 1848. She became the college's first woman tutor in mathematics. As head teacher of Cheltenham Ladies College from 1858, she turned the school into one of the most highly regarded in the country, switching the emphasis from traditional female subjects, such as music, needlework and drawing, to more academic disciplines.

Emily Faithfull, shown here (bottom left) in a photograph taken in about 1890, was an active campaigner for women who made a series of lecture tours in the 1870s. Her aim was to 'seek remunerative employment for women'. She wanted women to be given the chance to take up a trade or profession on the same terms as men. She set up the Victoria Press, a printing and publishing works staffed solely by women. The all-male union of printers was not impressed, condemning her 'obnoxious scheme'.

Millicent Fawcett (right) was a pioneer advocate of votes for women. She was the younger sister of the groundbreaking woman doctor, Elizabeth Garret, and one of the founders of Newnham College in 1871. She later became president of the National Union of Women's Suffrage Societies. Her husband was Henry Fawcett, Professor of Political Economy at Cambridge and the Liberal MP for Brighton. He had every sympathy for her cause. Together with John Stuart Mill, he tried, unsuccessfully, to persuade the House of Commons to grant women the right to vote.

and Cambridge resolutely refused to allow women to take actual degrees. Nor were women considered capable of studying Latin and Greek.

In 1880, an American student at Girton called Charlotte Scott was given a special dispensation to sit for the mathematical Tripos with her male Cambridge contemporaries. She came an extremely creditable eighth in the examination. Had she been a man, the university would have awarded her the title of 'eighth wrangler', but being a woman meant she was automatically disqualified. Her friends decided not to let such an obvious injustice pass without protest. When the name of the male wrangler who had taken her eighth position was read out in the Senate House, a party of Charlotte's supporters began a determined, though decorous, chant of 'Scott of Girton! Scott of Girton!'.

continued on page 155

WRITERS AND ARTISTS

Victorians loved novels. Some authors – notably Dickens, Trollope and George Eliot – earned fortunes from them. But they were the lucky few. The majority of writers, especially poets, found it difficult to make ends meet. On the whole, painters – such as Alma-Tadema, Holman Hunt, Landseer, Leighton and Millais – earned far more than their literary counterparts. Having hit on a saleable formula, some artists stuck to it like glue. Thomas Sidney Cooper, who painted contented cows and demure sheep, boasted he could finish two such pictures 'every morning before breakfast'.

OLD AND NEW
Robert Browning (above) was better known for his runaway elopement with fellow writer Elizabeth Barrett than for his poetry until relatively late in his career. Many found his verse hard to follow; Tennyson said that he only understood the first and last lines of 'Sordello'. Oscar Wilde (left) studied at Trinity College, Dublin, and at Oxford before moving to London, where he quickly made his mark on the literary scene. Gilbert and Sullivan satirised him as Reginald Bunthorne, the 'fleshly poet' in *Patience*.

NORTH OF THE BORDER
John Stuart Blackie (right) was one of the best-known Scotsmen of his day. He fought almost singlehandedly to preserve the Gaelic language, raising the funds needed to endow a new Chair of Celtic at Edinburgh University, where he was Professor of Greek. Blackie was a flamboyant figure in private as well as public life. 'Watch him as he struts up and down a lecture platform', wrote a Glasgow journalist in 1877, 'giving out his sharp, witty, egotistical sayings and keeping the audience in a roar.'

'I write for money. Of course I do. It is for money that we all work, lawyers, publishers, authors and the rest.'

Anthony Trollope

ARTS AND CRAFTSMAN

William Morris (left) is best remembered today for his wallpaper designs (opposite, bottom left and right). In the multi-talented manner of the age, Morris painted, wrote poetry, translated ancient classics and became a founder of the socialist movement. Above all, he valued quality of craftsmanship, which is amply illustrated by the furniture and fabrics in this bedroom at Kelmscott Manor (above), from 1869 his country home near Lechlade in Oxfordshire. Like the Pre-Raphaelites, Morris was greatly influenced by medieval art and he formed a company with Gabriel Rossetti, Ford Madox Brown and Edward Burne-Jones, among others, to promote fine workmanship in furnishings and domestic art. The inlaid settle (right) was made by the company to a design by Philip Webb.

DESIGNED TO LAST

The influence of William Morris's Arts and Crafts movement was still to reach its height, but his work and designs were already popular by the 1870s. His manufacturing company began the decade by the name of Morris, Marshall, Faulkner & Co, and the angel above is an example of its stained glass, produced for a window in 1870 to a design by Rossetti and Burne-Jones. By 1875 the company was under Morris's sole ownership as Morris & Co. For the rest of the decade he concentrated increasingly on fabrics – the bird design (right) was for a tapestry. Typically, he went back to first principles, studying the traditional art of dyeing before immersing himself in textile production.

THE FEMALE TOUCH

Elizabeth Thompson (far right) married a general and became Lady Elizabeth Butler. She was an acclaimed painter of military themes, even though she never actually witnessed any of the events she depicted. Queen Victoria commissioned her to paint a picture commemorating the gallantry of the defenders of Rorke's Drift in the otherwise less-than-glorious Zulu War.

Eliza Cook (right) published her own journal, a weekly magazine that, in her own words, was full of 'utility and amusement'. She also wrote poetry. Her poem 'The Old Armchair' was so popular it made her a household name in Britain and America. The critic for the *New York Times* was not one of her fans, describing her verses as 'silly'.

PORTRAIT PAINTER

Hailing from a family of painters, George Richmond (right) started his artistic career as a disciple of William Blake. With Samuel Palmer, his closest friend, and Edward Calvert, he founded 'The Ancients', a group of artists dedicated to painting visionary works in the manner of their great master. Richmond went on to become one of the Victorian era's most prolific portraitists.

ESTABLISHED ARTIST

Richard Redgrave (right), a landscape and genre painter, was a pillar of the artistic establishment. He ended up as Inspector-General of Art at the Victoria & Albert Museum, which he had helped to found, and Surveyor of the Queen's Pictures. But not all of his fellow artists had respect for the man. Whistler, for one, cordially disliked him. The prosperous Redgrave is seen here at home in his lavish studio. He is wearing what generally became recognised as the standard artist's uniform – velvet jacket and embroidered cap. Art was fast becoming respectable, although in social terms much of the transformation was skin-deep. Many artists were quick to climb up the social ladder. Landseer, for one, affected an aristocratic drawl 'till it became a second nature'.

SPINE TINGLER

As the author of so-called 'sensational novels' – most famously *The Woman in White* (published 1860) and *The Moonstone* (1868) – Wilkie Collins (left) was one of the best-known and best-paid writers of the day. He had started out as a lawyer, but turned to journalism and writing after his father's death, having first toyed with the idea of becoming a painter. His star began to wane after the death of Charles Dickens, his friend and mentor for two decades. In his works of the 1870s Collins began to tackle social issues and his readership deserted him. His popularity as an author never recovered.

PESSIMISTIC PROSE

Matthew Arnold (far left) was a poet and critic, and one of the most influential essayists of the period. In common with Thomas Carlyle (left), he was deeply opposed to change. He condemned scientific advance, for instance, as symbolic of the onward march of the Philistine middle-classes. Carlyle was an intellectual giant. He had won renown at an early age with his classic account of the French Revolution. But later in life he opposed extending the right to vote and what he saw as a seemingly inevitable drift towards democracy, a trend that he called 'swamery'.

THE RISE OF THE GREETING CARD

YE MERRIE CHRISTMASSE TIME

YE FAMILY STIRABOUTE

A glad NEW YEAR

All that makes life sweet and dear
Come to thee to bless the Year.

A bell in shape, a belle in beauty too,
I'd like a little belle like you,
Your pretty tinting would amuse my life
If you'd allow me to ring you for wife.

A glad NEW YEAR

All that makes life sweet and dear
Come to thee to bless the Year.

If it should snow on New Year's day

At home dear friend you'd better stay

MERRY CHRISTMAS!
This selection of cards from the 1870s includes Christmas cards, New Year cards and Valentine cards, irrefutable evidence of the growth of a major new industry. *The Times* described the card business as having 'opened up a new field of labour for artists, lithographers, engravers, printers, and ink and pasteboard makers'.

Although the practice of sending cards was only introduced around two decades earlier, by 1878 some 4.5 million Christmas cards were posted in Britain – and about the same number of cards were sent for Valentine's Day. A huge variety of designs appeared to meet the rising demand. Some featured fairy-tale or folk characters, while others were comical. Some were heavily embossed or decorated with silk fringes, tassels and cords. For Christmas, what are now considered traditional seasonal symbols – plum pudding, holly, mistletoe and the ubiquitous Christmas tree – were all becoming firm favourites.

UNSTOPPABLE STEAM
A lone bystander watches a crack east coast express train power its way north in 1875. In the 1870s, the east coast route was controlled by three different companies. From King's Cross in London to Doncaster the line was owned by the Great Northern Railway. From Doncaster to the Scottish border was the property of the North Eastern Railway. Then north through Scotland it was run by the North British Railway.

The rise of the railways continued with unstoppable momentum. By 1875 more than 500 million passenger journeys were being made by rail each year. Trains were becoming more comfortable – although even expresses still did not have corridors linking the coaches – and they were also getting faster. It was estimated that it took less time to travel by rail from London Bridge Station to Brighton than it took to get from London Bridge to Paddington via London's roads.

THE TAY BRIDGE DISASTER

The 1870s had opened with Britain in confident, almost ebullient mood. But despite the obvious progress that had been made in social and political reforms, the decade closed in growing doubt and uncertainty. Then, at the very end of 1879, a disaster occurred that shocked the whole nation. The British had come to trust and rely on their railways, but British engineering supremacy, for so long accepted as an unchallengeable fact, was called into question on the stormy night of 28 December, 1879. In gale-force winds gusting up to 70 miles an hour, the central spans of the new rail bridge across the Firth of Tay at Dundee collapsed without warning. The Edinburgh to Dundee mail train was on the bridge at the time. Unable to stop, it plunged into the icy river, taking with it all 75 passengers, none of whom survived.

The Tay railway bridge had been hailed as yet another triumph of British engineering when it opened just 18 months before. It was designed by Thomas Bouch, one of the most celebrated engineers of the day, who had been knighted by the Queen for his work on the project. At nearly two miles long, the bridge was the longest of its kind in the world. It was also the single largest engineering project undertaken in Britain. The bridge had consisted of 85 spans, 72 of which were supported on spanning girders and slender cast iron columns, braced with wrought iron struts and ties, below the level of the railway track. The remaining 13 spans – the 'high girders' as they were known – were above track level. It was these girders that fell, taking the Edinburgh train to its doom.

The enquiry

A Board of Trade enquiry was quickly convened to investigate the catastrophic collapse. It came to the stark conclusion that Thomas Bouch was primarily to blame for not having made adequate allowance in his calculations for the wind pressure that would be brought to bear on the structure in gale-force conditions. He had allowed for wind pressure of 10 pounds a square foot. 'The fall of the bridge,' the enquiry team reported, 'was occasioned by the insufficiency of the cross bracing and its fastenings to sustain the force of the gale.' The enquiry concluded that, had the piers and the wind bracing been properly constructed, the bridge in all probability could have withstood the storm.

Bouch was a broken man. He died shortly after the report was published, but he was not the only one who came in for censure. Hopkins, Gilkes & Co, the Teesside construction company that built the bridge, was heavily criticised and went bankrupt as a result. 'The great object', the enquiry commented, 'seems to have been to get through the work with as little delay as possible without seeing whether it was properly and carefully executed or not.'

Recorded for posterity

One man was made famous by the disaster, although in all probability that was not his intention. William McGonagall, the self-proclaimed 'poet laureate of the

AFTERMATH

In January 1880, there was only one news story. *The Illustrated London News* led with a bleak picture of the wrecked Tay Bridge. Founded in 1842, *The Illustrated London News* was the world's first illustrated newspaper. Its mission, it proudly proclaimed, was 'to keep continuously before the eye of the world a living and moving panorama of all its activities and influences'. Photographs were not yet in general use in the paper, but the illustration well conveys the horror of the bridge's collapse into the raging waters of the Firth. As the news broke, *The Times* reported how 'strong men and women are wringing their hands in despair' as a fruitless search for survivors began. Everyone on the train perished. Diving operations to locate the wreckage started almost immediately. The steam engine that was pulling the fateful train – ironically named *The Diver* – was eventually retrieved (right). It was subsequently repaired and continued working until 1919, when it was finally retired and scrapped.

silvery Tay', penned a poem lamenting the disaster and it made him a household name. The poem is undoubtedly one of the worst ever written – although some of McGonagall's other poetic concoctions run it very close. He set the tone in his opening lines:

> 'Beautiful Railway Bridge of the Silv'ry Tay,
> Alas! I am very sorry to say,
> That ninety lives have been taken away,
> On the last Sabbath Day of 1879,
> Which will be remembered for a very long time …'

On and on the poem rambled, until it reached its concluding couplets and delivered McGonagall's moral:

> 'I must now conclude my lay,
> By telling the world fearlessly without the least dismay,
> That your central girders would not have given way.
> At least many sensible men do say,
> Had they been supported on each end by buttresses,
> At least many sensible men confess,
> For the stronger we our houses do build,
> The less chance we have of being killed.'

The piers that once supported the great iron columns remain standing in the river to this day, a grim reminder of that terrible December night in 1879. A new decade now beckoned, and few could have possibly predicted the dramatic changes and developments that it would bring.

'So the train moved slowly along the Bridge of Tay,
Until it was about midway,
Then the central girders with a crash gave way,
And down went the train and passengers
    into the Tay!'

William McGonagall

INDEX

PICTURE ACKNOWLEDGEMENTS

Abbreviations: t = top; m = middle; b = bottom; r = right; c = centre; l = left

All images in this book are courtesy of Getty Images, including the following which have additional attributions:
12-13, 19tl, 19mr, 112br, 146t, 146b: Time & Life Pictures
41, 43, 65, 69b, 129, 130, 131, 142-143: Sean Sexton
86, 87t, 93b, 97b, 134, 144b, 153bm: Popperfoto
89t: Imagno
98: George Eastman House
148br, 149: Bridgeman Art Library

LOOKING BACK AT BRITAIN
HOLIDAYS AND HARD TIMES – 1870s
is published by The Reader's Digest Association Ltd, London, in association with Getty Images and Endeavour London Ltd.

Copyright © 2009 The Reader's Digest Association Ltd

The Reader's Digest Association Ltd
11 Westferry Circus
Canary Wharf
London E14 4HE
www.readersdigest.co.uk

Endeavour London Ltd
21–31 Woodfield Road
London W9 2BA
info@endeavourlondon.com

Written by
Jeremy Harwood

For Endeavour
Publisher: Charles Merullo
Designer: Tea Aganovic
Picture editor: Jennifer Jeffrey
Production: Mary Osborne

For Reader's Digest
Project editor: Christine Noble
Art editor: Conorde Clarke
Indexer: Marie Lorimer
Proofreader: Ron Pankhurst
Pre-press account manager: Dean Russell
Product production manager: Claudette Bramble
Production controller: Sandra Fuller

Reader's Digest General Books
Editorial director: Julian Browne
Art director: Anne-Marie Bulat

Colour origination by Chroma Graphics Ltd, Singapore
Printed and bound in China

We are committed both to the quality of our products and the service we provide to our customers. We value your comments, so please do contact us on 08705 113366 or via our website at
www.readersdigest.co.uk

If you have any comments or suggestions about the content of our books, email us at
gbeditorial@readersdigest.co.uk

CONCEPT CODE: UK 0154/L/S
BOOK CODE: 638-005 UP0000-1
ISBN: 978 0 276 44393 0
ORACLE CODE: 356900005H.00.24